Endorsements

This book offers a lovely, compelling vision of the church of the future—a church that is focused on God's reign and our chance to participate in advancing it. I am so glad to know that thoughtful leaders like Ulrick Refsager Dam will help lead the way!

—**Rev. Dr. David P. Gushee**, Author of "After Evangelicalism"

Grappling with issues of faith and belief has become somewhat commonplace in these times of upheaval. The impact of digitality and an increasingly interconnected and globalized world has presented immense challenges to traditional beliefs. This book is a bold attempt to wrestle with how, and in what ways, those who are struggling to keep their 'spiritual heads' above water might find pathways to a vibrant future, personally and within their communities.

—**Barry Taylor**, theologian and author of "Sex, God, and Rock'n'Roll"

With so many leaving the church today, Ulrick Refsager Dam's new book, Building the Basileia: Moving the Church on to the 22nd Century, is a realistic, relevant attempt to call them back. This book sets the stage for critical change necessary in our churches today. Beginning with Open and Relational Theology, Dam takes the next practical step and translates ORT into Open and Relational Ecclesiology. He provides a glimpse into how we might not only build the church but, more importantly, partner with God to promote the well being of all God's creation. Dam writes, "Faith is an activator, which sets us out on a journey, with the vision of healing and rebuilding all of creation, starting with the given Church's own neighborhood." I highly recommend this book for all who desire to be a partner with God in this change.

—**Deanna M. Young**, DThM, Author of Unblaming God: Interpreting the Old Testament Through the Lens of Jesus Christ; Elder UMC

This book is a wonderful demonstration of how theology can be done not merely to enrich an emerging academic field (which it undoubtedly accomplishes) but also to serve the life of the church. Dam breaks new ground developing an ecclesiology within Open and Relational Theology, and he does so combining scholarly depth with accessible clarity.

—**Martin Jakobsen**, Associate professor in systematic theology, Ansgar University College

The church has, since Paul, marked its purpose as making known the one who the ancient Athenians called the 'agnostos theos'. Paul interpreted this to mean, 'the unknown God', which was, no doubt, the intended meaning of those who coined the term. Yet, there is a much more radical interpretation which may well define the purpose of the church should it undergo—as it needs to—a new Reformation. The shape of Future Church will be decided by discussions around, not the unknown God, but the Unknowing God. The Next Reformation will be marked, not by the logic of the 'not-all', where God is an exception to the deterministic universe, but rather by the logic of the 'non-all', where God and the universe share in a radical openness. Central to this vital conversation is the battle between open and radical theology. In this excellent work, Ulrick Dam makes the case for open theology in an accessible and engaging way. Whilst I ultimately take my stand with radical theology, if anyone were to convince me otherwise, it would be Ulrick.

—**Peter Rollins**, philosopher and theologian. Author of "How (not) to speak of God" and "The Divine Magician"

To look around at the state of affairs in Western Christianity today is to gaze upon a historical moment of a church who wants a future but seemingly doesn't have one. Between polarizing rhetoric that refuses change, to a God that has evidently been outmoded and outwitted by digitality and technology, to buildings that are falling a part, funds that are drying up, and people finding a sense of community and belonging in a myriad of other places, how can the modern day church compete? This book offers a way forward past the antiquated conversations towards new questions of God, community, and transformation. In a time when so many are asking what might be left of Christianity, here we are presented with a thoughtful, developed, theologically sound, and biblically attuned offering.

—**Maria Francesca French**, post-christian thinker and theologian. Author of "Safer than the known way"

This new book is full of inspiring invitation and thoughtful theology. It reorients our view of the redemptive work of the church in the world as we bear witness to and participate with Christ in the redemption and restoration of all things. I'm thrilled to have a front row seat to that work through leaders like Ulrick, and his colleagues cultivating a compelling vision for faith communities today.

Keri Ladouceur, Co-founder and Executive Director, Post Evangelical Collective

ULRICK REFSAGER DAM

BUILDING THE BASILEIA

Moving the Church into the 22nd century

SacraSage

Print: 978-1-958670-18-7
Ebook: 978-1-958670-17-0

Printed in the United States of America

Library of Congress Cataloguing-in-Publication Data
SacraSage Press / Ulrick Refsager Dam

This book is dedicated to all my friends,
who's been cut off and thrown out of communities,
for stating the obvious, reflecting, and raising a
banner for those who could not.

_____

*For we are co-workers in God's service; you are
God's field, God's building.*

—Pauls First Letter to the Corinthians 3:9 (NIV)

Contents

PART TWO

Open and Relational Theology

PART THREE

Open and Relational Ecclesiology

PART FOUR

Finishing Remarks

Foreword

Open and relational theology comes in many forms. Because it fits everyday experience, however, open and relational theology makes a great deal of sense as practical theology. It fits life as we know it.

Take prayer as an example. Most of us pray thinking our activity makes a difference to God. We believe the future may be different because we prayed. But most traditional theologies portray God as outside time and unaffected by anything we do. In them, prayer doesn't matter. Open and relational theology thinks otherwise, and it fits the common practice of petitionary prayer.

Or take sin and evil. Most people think things happen that make our lives and the world worse. God is not pleased when we harm ourselves, others, or the earth. These occurrences are not what God wants or part of some timeless divine plan. But most conventional theologies portray God as operating from a predetermined blueprint. In their view, whatever occurs—righteous or unrighteous—is part of God's plan. Open and relational theology says otherwise.

Let me offer one more example. The apostle Paul compares a healthy church to a body of interrelated and mutually influencing parts. Christ is the head of this body, both influencing it and being influenced by it. No part should say to another, "I don't need you," because all play a valuable role to making the body healthy. That's a central tenet in open and relational theology.

Ulrick Refsager Dam gets it right in this book. In this creative and important work, Ulrick offers an open and relational, practical theology of ecclesiology. And it's rich and provocative. I suspect some readers will come upon passages and say, "Of course, who would think otherwise?" The best practices in practical theology fit hand-in-glove with open and relational thinking. And yet few people know about this natural fit. This book should help many realize that Christian piety makes sense in this theological perspective.

I offer a prediction: I predict the book you are holding will spark further engagement in open and relational ecclesiology. Ulrick's offerings will alter the open and relational landscape. As you read, in fact, I encourage you to ask, "How might I contribute to the life-giving work to match practice with theory, piety with reflection, or the church and the academy?"

Let this fine book spark creative rumination!

Thomas Jay Oord

Preface

Listen, I have never been a big fan of prefaces to books. Usually, I skim through or straight up skip them. All of that is just to say: I will keep this part short and sweet!

This book came into being because of my love for Open and Relational Theology. But I lacked something! So much of Open and Relational Theology is founded in systematic thinking. We have great books diving into any dogmatic issue you can think of. But we miss books that help us to actively and practically build communities built on Open and Relational Theology.

That is why I wrote this book.

Actually, that is why I used my thesis time when studying for a Master's in Leadership and Congregational Development to take the first steps towards evolving an Open and Relational Ecclesiology. This book is based on that thesis.

The book is divided into three parts: Firstly, we shall look at what defines ecclesiology. Secondly, I will present Open and Relational Theology to you. Thirdly, we shall look towards an Open and Relational Ecclesiology.

I hope this will be an inspiration and a help to your practical work and leadership.

Enjoy,
Ulrick

Acknowledgements

"No man is an island entire of itself; every man is a piece of the continent."

—JOHN DONNE (1624)

This book only became a reality, due to the blessings of great friends, family, acquaintances, colleagues, and so many more. I am entirely grateful that you all helped me, stood with me, and carried me forward. And know that I am thankful for all of you.

There are a few individuals who are completely essential for the becoming of this book:

- My beloved Grandmother, who taught me that you do not have to live on the terms the life deals you. You can choose to walk your own path and choose to be joyous each day.
- My loving wife, Sara, who never reads a word of anything I write and who never listens to my sermons or teachings. It is a blessing to have a secure home base where no one listens to your theological meanderings. Thank you! (Even though you'll probably never know I wrote this)

- Thomas Oord, who has a peculiar gift for telling people that they are clearly Open and Relational Theologians, even though they do not know it themselves. Thanks for setting me on this path.

Introduction

Theology can have a bad reputation in some charismatic circles. *We don't do theology. We are disciples following Jesus*, some might say. What these people do not realize is that their very attitude toward theology loudly speaks of their view of God and, therefore, their own theology.

I want to start my book by recognizing that theology is not simply an academic discipline presented in dissertations and dusty old books. I want to start by recognizing that everything we do is, in some sense, theology. All our actions present our view of God and, therefore, our theology.

Consequently, theology must always be in focus in our Christian communities and the life of our congregations. All our actions present our view of God, but this is also true in the reverse order. Our thinking of God, which is, of course, our theology, also shapes our actions. There is a back-and-forth action between the two. We can say that theology will always shape our lives, just as it is shaped by our lives. Therefore, it becomes vital to always hold our theology in focus, letting it evolve and unfold, as well as shape us as Christians, without the theology becoming an idol that is worshiped and takes all the focus away from being disciples of Christ.

The American process theologian and Professor of Constructive Theology Catherine Keller wisely presents that theology is more than just words. At the beginning of her book *On the Mystery*, she acknowledges that theology is neither God talking through us nor is it our talk about God as if God is some sort of object that we can know fully. She writes, "Theology signifies something more: theology is a way of discerning divinity in process. The process is both that of our faith seeking understanding—and of that which we seek to understand."[1] All our actions speak loudly of how we view God and how we discern the process of divinity. In other words, to Keller, theology comes through seeking a deeper relationship with God. And the deeper our relation with God, the more it shapes our being.

Theology, then, is an ever-evolving process of trying to move closer to God in the relationship and also a process of making sense of the world and God in the context of our lived reality. This also emphasizes that theology speaks of a reality greater than our own; it points toward an ultimate state of creation. Therefore, we, as Christians, are called to be *in, but not of* this world.[2] Or rather, God chose us to be *out of this world,* as is the correct quote from the Gospel of John. As Christians, we are called to point the world toward the deep reality of God and not just mere surface values.

The American philosopher and comparative theologian Philip Clayton puts it like this: Christians should be "a people that are 'in but not of' the world. Because our identity is not shaped 'by' the world, we can live 'for' it. Our calling is to be a people who, in cooperation with God's Spirit, seek to bring about an order of love and justice that is clearly not the world we see around us."[3] We Christians should always seek to further our knowledge

---

1. Catherine Keller, *On the Mystery: Discerning Divinity in Process* (Minneapolis, MN: Fortress Press, 2008), 24–25.

2. John 15:18-19

3. Philip Clayton and Tripp Fuller, *Transforming Christian Theology: For Church and Society* (Minneapolis: Fortress Press, 2010), 16.

and deepen our understanding of God and how God acts in this world. This is a lifelong process in which we will never find ultimate answers, only further and deeper questions. As creation evolves, so does our knowledge and experience of God.

To draw the lines sharply, very few people today, if any, believe in an actual three-tiered universe where God floats around on a cloud with pearly gates. We have been above the clouds, and we have even been deep inside the earth. Nowhere did we find heaven or hell. This knowledge forces us to develop our theology. In the same way, women's rights forced us to rethink much of Paul's writing. All this development furthers and deepens our understanding of God and how God works. Developing new theology not only makes our Christian faith relevant in a new day and age, but it also helps us to understand the kingdom that God is building.

This book seeks to dive deeper into and explore how we can understand God today. As I said, it is essential to always evolve our theology, considering the knowledge of our present day. The deeper we allow the questions to dig, the higher our knowledge and wisdom will soar, and the wiser and more well-rounded our theology will become.

In this book, you and I will be hiking into mostly uncharted areas to try to define Open and Relational Ecclesiology (ORE). The whole arena of Open and Relational Theology (ORT) is relatively new and, therefore, still has many largely uncharted areas. Ecclesiology is one of them. Hiking into areas of uncharted practical theology is an important task! Evolving new practical theology that is fitting to the day and age is important. It has the main purpose of helping and correcting the church, calling out trends that could be destructive, and drawing the church back to the calling from God. John Swinton and Harriet Mowat point to this in the introduction of their book *Practical Theology and Qualitative Method*. They note that "[o]ne of the main critical tasks of Practical

Theology is to recognize distorted practice and to call the Church back to the theological significance of its practices and to enable it to engage faithfully with the mission of God." They say the sole purpose of practical theology is to call the church back into the mission of God, guiding it back on track, focusing on what is important, and correcting distorted practices. In this book, I will make my contribution by calling out some distorted practices of the church and offering practical aspects to call the church back into the mission of God through the definitions of ORE.

In my definition, ORE must rest on two theological legs: Firstly, that the church is in, but not of, the world. This leg takes seriously that the church is working to instate the Basileia in co-operation with the Divine, that the future is open, and that we must act in accordance. The second theological leg is a continual call to be partners in the creation process. Christianity is meant to be an active faith that motivates and guides us to constantly build a better world and care for all of creation. This leads us to three practical outputs: Firstly, we must focus the work of the church on serving more than doing services. In other words, we must act out our role as co-creators. Secondly, the church must work to lead in the same way that God leads us, and as we see Jesus leading in scripture, namely utilizing relational leadership, where we seek to build up the character and very being of each other. The third practical output is the need for radical inclusiveness in the church. As all humans are the beloved children of God and as all are in the presence of God, then all must be welcomed and accepted as part of our divine family, no matter who, what, or where they are on their journey with God.

The call of practical theology also means that we constantly need to develop and evolve our theology. Theologies are equally a description of our worldview as well as an effort to describe our understanding of God. In our world today, everything is evolving and changing at the speed of light. We know some of the most intimate secrets of the universe, yet we have not found God sitting somewhere on a tiny particle or above a cloud. The more we know of the universe, the more our understanding of God evolves, expands, and needs to be adjusted. Evolving new theologies makes talking of God and framing our lived experience within the biblical narrative relevant for us today.

In the same way, we must recognize that humankind has evolved since Jesus walked this earth. Our understanding and knowledge have evolved, and therefore, our conceptions of God have evolved as well. Theologian Herbert A. Youtz most poetically says, "The savage man has a savage God; the cruel man has a cruel God; the effeminate man has an effeminate God; while the good man lifts up holy hands to a God who rewards goodness."[4]

Our image of God shapes and forms us, just as our way of living shapes our view of God. There is an inherent back-and-forth action between the two. As humankind evolves, so does our theology and culture, and so does our view of God and our understanding of God. This is where ORT steps in: as a theology that wants to make sense of our understanding of God in this very day and age and helps us move toward a better future for the church.

All in all, I hope that open and relational ecclesiology can help us to lay the foundation for moving the church forward and start looking toward the 22nd century.

1.1 What is the focus?

This book is based on the thesis I wrote for my Master's in Leadership and Congregational Development at Ansgar School of Theology and Mission. I wrote my thesis to contribute to the

---

4. Herbet A. Youtz, 'Three Conceptions of God', *American Journal of Theology* II (1907): 428.

field of open and relational theology. In rewriting the thesis into this book, I have tried to focus more and make this material practically applicable. I want you, my reader, to be inspired and to evolve your thinking and practice of ecclesiology. Throughout the book, there will be parts that are more academically minded, but we will end up with practically applicable knowledge.

The field of open and relational theology is a rather new concept that has been sprouting forth within the last 30 years. The American theologian Thomas Jay Oord can be seen as the main man behind open and relational theology, which is a term that he has coined.[5] This new branch of theology bases itself on process philosophy and open theism, as well as draws on thinkers like Whitehead, Wesley, and Kierkegaard.

Open and relational theology stands on two main theological pillars: the belief that God is open, which means that God does not foreknow the future and that God experiences time moment by moment together with all of creation, and the belief that God is relational, meaning God truly wants real relationships with all of creation. I will expand on this later in the book, but for now, I will shortly explain why the words *open* and *relational* are important.

Open is often explained by looking at God as a jazz band-leader. God does not have the entire session planned out like a classical composer has, meaning God does not have one plan for how the future will be but is open to creaturely cooperation and experiences time moment by moment together with the rest of creation. God does not foreknow the future but is open to the band's movement, like the jazz bandleader. There is no settled future for the current session. There is, of course, a desired outcome: a beautiful piece of music where all cooperate to piece together

---

5. Thomas Jay Oord, *Open and Relational Theology: An Introduction to Life-Changing Ideas* (Grasmere, Idaho: SacraSage Press, 2021).

the musical components. It is not just complete chaos but a process that points toward a common goal and ending. Together, the band and the leader create beautiful music. "Like an inspiring jazz band leader," as Oord says, "a Guide nudges, gestures, and coaxes us toward creative expression. This Leader experiences the music as it happens, along with everyone else, uncertain where the tune will go. It's experimental, not prearranged."[6]

The bandleader guides and nudges us into the best plan of events. But we are free musicians who can play what we want to. The tune is still uncertain, even as we are nudged toward a greater purpose!

ORT argues against notions of Calvinist predestination and classical notions of a perfect, timeless God. According to ORT, God experiences time moment by moment together with all of creation and does not foreknow the future. If God did, we would not be able to be truly free because all of our actions would either already be settled in God's plans for the future or, through God's foreknowing of the future and all of our future actions, would *de facto* be settled.

Relational means that God can be genuinely affected by creation. ORT argues against the classical notions of God's impassibility and immutability. Impassibility means that God would be incapable of feeling emotions. ORT argues that God is highly capable of emotions and feels all of creation. Immutability means that God is incapable of changing. ORT argues that God changes and evolves. We pray to God and have a real relationship with God because it affects God and helps God's experience to change and evolve together with all of creation. This means we live in a giving-and-receiving relationship with God. Oord writes,

Consider our day-to-day relationship with God. It's impossible to have give-and-receive relations with an impassible and

---

6. Oord, 28.

invulnerable deity. He can't respond to prayer, for instance, and isn't happy when we love or feel sad when we suffer. An impassible God could never console those who grieve. The unaffected God is an emotionless stick in the mud.[7]

Scholars and thinkers within ORT argue that God must be relational and affected by time to be able to respond to our prayers and to be in a real give-and-take relationship with creation. They also argue that this is a more scriptural understanding than the classic notions of God.

ORT is, as said, a relatively new movement. In the past years, many books have been published in areas such as Christology, pneumatology, soteriology, and prayer within the context of ORT. However, one field is mostly untouched: open and relational ecclesiology. To the best of my knowledge, no real work has been done on ORE, although there have been some publications on the fringes of ecclesiology. One notable example is an anthology of short essays on ORT and leadership from 2020. The book *Leading with Love* was a collection of snapshots of different leaders' own reflections on leadership and ORT.[8] This was a good contribution but not one that works more academically to define ORE. In this book, I am pursuing to explore, in a more academic way, how God's openness and relatedness change and affect our congregations and Churches, leadership, and so on. But this is not only for academic purposes. I want to contribute to the practical life of churches today. And I believe ORE can be a great tool for that!

So, while ORT has been quickly storming forth within theological circles, I see that there are still many uncharted areas. While a great amount of research and scholarship has been put

---

7. Oord, 52.

8. Roland Hearn, Sheri D. Kling, and Thomas Jay Oord, eds., *Open and Relational Leadership - Leading with Love* (USA: Sacra Sage, 2020).

into defining many systematic aspects of ORT, such as proper theology, Christology, soteriology, and eschatology, many of the practical aspects of ORT have largely been neglected. Some work has been done with ORT and pastoral care and social justice issues, but none have actually tried to form an ecclesiology. This is, of course, not due to ill-will of the practical theological aspect but simply due to ORT being initially approached as a philosophical and systematic concept. Due to its freshness, no work has yet been done on many of the practical aspects, as not many communities have adopted ORT.

That is exactly where this book steps in. In this book, I will investigate ORE and explore what ORT means for the life of congregations and Churches and how it could affect leadership, values, and organization.

In my thesis, that led me to use the following research question: *How may an Open and Relational Ecclesiology be formulated, and how would it come to live in a congregational setting?* That is the main focus of this book as well: to try and formulate, or at least take the first couple of steps toward ORE.

To explore this field, we must first look at what defines ecclesiology. We will do that by looking at two different takes on ecclesiology: first, from Avery Cardinal Dulles and then from Jürgen Moltmann. From there, we can explore what distinguishes open and relational theology. Finally, we can start taking the first small steps toward how we could formulate an open and relational ecclesiology.

In this book, I will try to explore some of the ways that ORE can be of benefit to our everyday life in Churches. I truly believe that ORT should not just be a discipline for the academically minded theologian but a theology that helps ministry in praxis. ORT has a real practical outlet, which could be embraced easily in many congregations, and that would have a positive effect on the life in those congregations. Therefore, I set out to explore just that! Will you walk with me on this journey?

1.2 So what can you expect?

This book is largely based on my master's thesis, which I finished in 2023. I wanted to dive into ORE and focus on how churches embraced ORT. It quickly became clear to me that not many churches completely embrace ORT. Sure, there are more pastors and church leaders who embrace ORT and work to affect their congregations in that way. However, the sample size of congregations who explicitly adhere to ORT was just too small. Therefore, I decided to do my thesis as a literature study. That means that I based the thesis on books, articles, and other writings from open and relational theologians and scholars, open theists, process philosophers, and others alike. In this way, I could create an overview of the basic steps needed to move toward ORE for pastors and leaders who would like to push their congregation in that direction.

Looking at the literature study, it is really not possible to completely lay out one single method for doing a literature study. The method can vary from different issues and different theologians. My method is shown in the structure of this book, in which I will first discuss what defines ecclesiology and afterward explore ORT. Combining my thoughts on ecclesiology and ORT will create a new discourse for ORE.

This book is divided into four parts:

- Part One, I will investigate ecclesiology and work to find key aspects of what defines ecclesiology. I will do this by looking at Avery Cardinal Dulles's typology of different Church models and add some perspective to this by drawing in Jürgen Moltmann's more Christ-centered ecclesiology.
- Part Two, I will work to define ORT. This is done mainly by laying out key aspects of ORT that will be important

to the definition of ORE. In defining ORT, I mainly look
toward the work of Thomas Jay Oord, who is the main
man in ORT and draw in other relevant thinkers.

- Part Three, I will work to define ORE based on the
introduction to ecclesiology and ORT.
- Part Four will round off the book with a short
perspectivation and conclusion.

Enjoy!

PART ONE

Ecclesiology

What is ecclesiology?

B efore we start exploring ORT, we need to look at what defines ecclesiology. At the most basic level, ecclesiology is the study of the Church and how it relates to Christ. This involves looking at the origins of Christianity, the Church's role in salvation, eschatology, how it is structured, how leadership works, and so on.

In early Christianity (the age of Paul and the first apostles), the primary practical ecclesiological issue was how to manage leadership and the status of Gentiles, etc. Later on, structures with councils, bishops, and hierarchy found their way into ecclesiology. Especially after Christianity became the Roman state religion and Church, ecclesiology revolved around the institutionalization of the Church. Today, ecclesiology is a vast arena that seeks to describe and evolve different denominations of the Christian Church. And with many opinions and theologies, ecclesiology increasingly becomes more and more complex.

The root of the word "ecclesiology" is the Greek word ἐκκλησία (ekklēsia), which means "congregation." Ecclesiology was coined in the 19th century, first appearing in the quarterly journal The British Critic in 1837. Naturally, it might have been used in this context for many years before this, but this is the earliest known

literature that mentions ecclesiology in a theological sense.[1] In
The British Critic, an anonymous contributor defines ecclesiology
as follows:

[A] science which may treat of the proper construction and op-
erations of the Church, or Communion, or Society of Christians;
and which may regard men as they are members of that society,
whether members of the Christian Church in the widest accep-
tation of the term, or members of some branch or communion
of that Church, located in some separate kingdom, and governed
according to its internal forms of constitution and discipline.[2]

Since then, some discussion has been of whether this was the
first time ecclesiology was defined. No matter what, it is a very
good, although very broad, definition. Ecclesiology is the study
of how to properly construct and operate the community of the
Church. Over the years, much studying and many definitions
have gone into ecclesiology. This means that ecclesiology is a very
vast area today. There is no singular definition or best practice
of ecclesiology. For this reason, we need to look at some models
of ecclesiology that can give us perspective on what to look for
in ORE.

In this part, I will start by examining Avery Cardinal Dulles's
models of the Church[3] as a basis for viewing the ecclesiological spectrum. From that, I will draw some connections to Jürgen
Moltmann's understanding of the Church, which clearly connects
ecclesiology to Christology and creates a strong focus on lived discipleship. This will be important for our later exploration of ORE.

---

1. Alister E. McGrath, ed., *The Blackwell Encyclopedia of Modern Christian Thought*,
Reprinted (Oxford: Blackwell, 2000), 127.

2. F. Rivington, *The British Critic and Quarterly Theological Review*, 1837, 220.

3. Avery Dulles, *Models of the Church*, Expanded ed (New York, NY: Image Books,
2002).

Dulles's models of the Church

To understand what defines ecclesiology, we can start by looking at Dulles's models of the Church. Avery Cardinal Dulles was a Jesuit priest and cardinal of the Catholic Church. Throughout his life, he did extensive work on ecclesiology and the development of the Church from the Catholic point of view. In 1978, Dulles first published his book *Models of the Church,* in which he defines five models of ecclesiology that describe different views of the Church structure. The five models are as follows:

1. The Church as Institution
2. The Church as Mystical Communion
3. The Church as Sacrament
4. The Church as Herald
5. The Church as Servant

Dulles manages to give a great overview and perspective of the width of the ecclesiological spectrum. For that reason, his work is a great place to start this discussion of ecclesiology. In the coming chapters, I will shortly outline each model.

3.1 The Church as Institution

Firstly, Dulles recognizes the Church as an institutionalized structure and starts by acknowledging that institutionalism is "a deformation of the true nature of the Church."[1] By this, Dulles means that all Churches, of course, have some degree of being an institution. When we have an organization or regular gathering of people, there will be a need for some structure and institution to not descend into complete chaos. But institutionalization is seen when the natural structure deforms into a centralization of power that blocks direct access from the Christian to Christ. To maintain this centralization, institutionalist ecclesiology has three main functions: teaching, sanctifying, and governing.[2] This structure sets the bishop as the main source of power in the Church. That means, according to Dulles, that the members of the Church are "in conscience bound to believe what the bishop declares."[3] What the bishop sanctifies is that which is holy. And we all stay within the governing of the bishop. For the Church as an institution to truly work, the Church needs its members to be "docile and obedient [and] rely on the ministration of the Church."[4]

In this sense, this model places the ministry as a communicator between Christians and Christ. This "barrier" between Christians and Christ can have negative side effects. In the Middle Ages, this made perfect sense, as the average Church member could not read the Bible or educate themselves. This is mostly not the case today, yet in some places today, this model still has its right, as it can

---

1. Dulles, 27.
2. Dulles, 29–30.
3. Dulles, 30.
4. Dulles, 34.

help people find Christ more through instruction than personal reflection.[5]

3.2 The Church as Mystical Communion

Secondly, Dulles defines the Church as a mystical communion "given by the Holy Spirit [that] finds expression in a network of mutual interpersonal relationships of concern and assistance."[6] Contrary to the Church as an institution, the Church as a mystical communion is not focused on hierarchical structures. Instead, it is a primarily interior community between God and the individual person. This communion is experienced internally rather than outwardly. However, it still needs a communal expression "by external bonds of creed, worship, and ecclesiastical fellowship,"[7] as Dulles puts it. In other words, the mystical communion does not seek its raison d'être in the outer structures. The focus of communion is making space for the graces and gifts of the Holy Spirit, a transforming union that is more intimate than anything we can describe in moral or juridical terms.[8] From that, the external bonds will naturally arise, expressed in worship and through the ecclesiastical fellowship. The Church, therefore, arises to service the structure of the mystical communion more than to govern it, as the institutionalized model would. The primary quality is the individual's experience of God in a fellowship of interpersonal relations, all seeking the Holy Spirit.

---

5. Dulles, 37.
6. Dulles, 42.
7. Dulles, 48.
8. Dulles, 49.

3.3 | The Church as Sacrament

Thirdly, Dulles looks at the Church as sacramental. Dulles starts by quoting the Jesuit priest and cardinal Henri de Lubac, who says, "If Christ is the sacrament of God, the Church is for us the sacrament of Christ,"[9] meaning that the Church is the full representation of Christ and makes Christ present in the world today. This is the main task of a sacrament: to be a sign of grace. Any sign, Dulles notes, could just point to something absent, but in this sense, the sacrament is different. The sacrament is more of a *full sign*, meaning a sign of something that is truly present with us today.[10] A sacrament is neither an individual action nor always socially constituted. We do not baptize ourselves or share the Eucharist alone. Dulles says that sacraments have a dialogic structure because "they take place in a mutual interaction that permits the people together to achieve the spiritual breakthrough that they could not achieve in isolation."[11] The sacrament becomes a communal symbol of the presence of grace in the group of people. In the same sense, the Church becomes a sign of the redeeming grace of Christ and signifies that there is grace given to anyone who accepts the invitation. The Church, therefore, is a sign of grace and becomes a sacrament.[12]

3.4 | The Church as Herald

Fourthly, Dulles names the Church as the herald of Christ. In spreading the gospel through the preached Word, the Church heralds the kingdom of Christ and points to an encounter with

---

9. Dulles, 56; Henri de Lubac, *Catholicism: Christ and the Common Destiny of Man* (San Francisco: Ignatius Press, 1988).

10. Dulles, *Models of the Church*, 58.

11. Dulles, 59.

12. Dulles, 60.

God.[13] The Church becomes constituted by the Word it preaches as an event where God addresses God's people and is believed by the people. Therefore, Dulles notes that the Church is "constituted by the word being proclaimed and faithfully heard."[14] This removes the deification from the Church—the Church is not the object of faith—and makes it a congregation that seeks to encounter the Holy Spirit.[15] The encounter is reached by preaching the Word into being in the congregation.

Preaching the gospel also becomes essential to salvation. Dulles says that preaching "summons men to put their faith in Jesus as Saviour [and] announces the day of salvation that is at hand for believers."[16] Preaching becomes an eschatological event that saves those who hear and believe and condemns those who do not believe. The Church heralds the gospel and invites everyone to believe in Christ as savior.

3.5 The Church as Servant

Fifthly, Dulles names the Church as servant for Christ and creation. Christ came to not only proclaim the Kingdom but to actually establish and realize the Kingdom by serving, healing, reconciling, etc. In the same way, the Church should serve Christ by continually building up the Kingdom of God in this world. Dulles, quoting Richard Cardinal Cushing, says, "The Lord was the 'man for others,' so must the Church be 'the community for others.'"[17] The focus of ecclesiology must then be to ser-

---

13. Dulles, 69.

14. Dulles, 69–70.

15. Dulles, 70.

16. Dulles, 76.

17. Richard Cardinal Cushing, *The Servant Church* (Boston: Daugthers of St. Paul, 1966), 8; Dulles, *Models of the Church*, 85.

vice the world around it and to build up that which was broken down. Therefore, it is essential that the Church must work with the structures of the world rather than building its own parallel structures.[18]

As God gave himself to the world through Christ, the whole world became the house of God, not just the singular Church. The Church must see itself as being a servant in a much larger house—the world. The Church lives in the world to be a servant to its master, Christ, and to live out his will in this world.[19] The focus is being a disciple, living in the footsteps of Jesus Christ, and continuing his work still today and in this world.

3.6 A summary of Dulles's models of the Church

These five models of the Church are a great place to start a discussion of ecclesiology. The first three models may be more relevant to a specific catholic context, but the last two models are significant in the contemporary Church, as we shall see later on.

I will now move on to draw in the ecclesiology of Jürgen Moltmann and try to make connections between Moltmann's strong focus on Christology and Dulles's models. These connections will be important to my discussion of ORE later.

---

18. Dulles, *Models of the Church*, 88.

19. Dulles, 88.

Moltmann's Christ-centered ecclesiology

Jürgen Moltmann may be one of the most influential contemporary theologians. Moltmann is set within German Reformed theology and has worked a lot with liberation theology. Moltmann is especially interesting in the context of ORT, as his views, in great part, would align with both the open and the relational aspects of ORT, even though Moltmann has never declared himself to be within the field of ORT. Moltmann's work on ecclesiology, with his clear focus on Christology, is very interesting in the view of ORT.

Now, to take a step back, what makes defining ecclesiology difficult is that it draws strings to all other parts of theology, to all the other -ologies, so to speak. This makes ecclesiology largely a Church political arena because it encompasses the entirety of theology. In other words, all of the other -ologies come to life and are shown through ecclesiology. Jürgen Moltmann puts it like this:

> A consistent theological doctrine of the Church is by its
> very nature an eminently political and social doctrine of
> the Church as well. It will link up the theological inter-
> pretation of the Church (doctrina de ecclesia) with the
> Church's politics (politia ecclesiatica) so that the conflicts
> become evident and the need to alter the Church's politics

in the light of the lordship of Christ can no longer be ignored.[1]

Moltmann places Christ as the center of ecclesiology. The theological doctrine of the Church must be a description of how the members of the community ought to live their lives so that they disciple Christ in the best possible way. This means that ecclesiology creates a back-and-forth motion between the members of the congregation and the clergy, where the lived lives of the congregation affect the clergy and vice versa.

In essence, Moltmann would say that we can see the ecclesiology expressed through the congregational members' lives and actions. Moltmann focuses on placing Christ in the center of ecclesiology and says ecclesiology should sprout from the discipleship of Christ: "it is in the interest of everyone who calls on the name of Christ to subordinate his own particular interests to 'Christ's' interest and hence, as Paul says, to 'live no longer for themselves but for him who for their sake died and was raised' (II Cor. 5.15)."[2] For the clergy, then, it becomes a task of laying out the life of Christ so that the congregation can live a life in line with this discipleship. This shows that there is an especially close connection between ecclesiology and Christology but also to all of the other -ologies. Moltmann goes on to point out just that: "In this respect, every Christian is a theologian. The theological interpretation of the Church does not divide; it is a bond that holds everything together in the all-embracing interest of Christ, which is common to all."[3] The lives of the members of the Church point to the understanding and interpretation of Christ. The way of

---

1. Jürgen Moltmann, *The Church in the Power of the Spirit: A Contribution to Messianic Ecclesiology*, 1st Fortress Press ed (Minneapolis: Fortress Press, 1993), 5–6.

2. Moltmann, 6.

3. Moltmann, 6.

being disciples of Christ shapes the life of the congregation, which is a communion of disciples of Christ.

As opposed to Dulles, this ecclesiology has a bottom-up approach. This means that Moltmann looks initially at the lived lives of the congregation to define what ecclesiology does. If one wants to work with ecclesiology, one needs to change the life of the congregation. Dulles views ecclesiology as more top-down, so the ecclesiology becomes a result of what the clergy decides to do with the Church.

One of the main dangers for all ecclesiologies, especially the ones working from a bottom-up perspective, is placing the main weight on the Church and not on Christ. Today, we see many Churches being led through modern-day organizational tools. We see Churches today that, for example, are being led with Lean, which focuses on optimizing the Church so that the activities that make the most profit are most highly valued. There are many good aspects of being more modern in leadership, but it also places the congregation in danger of pushing out Christ or leaving too little room for divine inspiration. Working ecclesiology through modern leadership tools can lead to placing the focus of the Church on making a profit instead of focusing on always following Christ. In the same way, structures and institutionalization can take up too much space in ecclesiology, where running the organization "Church" becomes the main focus instead of following Christ. Moltmann writes,

> The Church's first word is not 'Church' but Christ. The Church's final word is not 'Church' but the glory of the Father and the Son in the Spirit of liberty. Because of this the Church, as Ambrose said, is like the moon, which has no light of its own or for itself. If it is the true Church, the light that is reflected on its face is the light of Christ, which reflects the glory of God, and it shines on the face

of the Church for the people who are seeking their way to freedom in the darkness.[4]

The Church is first and foremost looking toward Christ and in every way trying to reflect Christ on to the world around it. For Moltmann, ecclesiology is essentially an expression of how the congregation reflects the Kingdom of God through following Christ. It is an expression of the difference between faith and experience.[5] The Church is, so to speak, what makes faith come to life. Through the biblical narrative, we can see a huge focus on community: that God is present in communal life. Jesus, in particular, places an enormous emphasis on community. He starts his work by calling disciples to fellowship. He sends his disciples out in pairs. He teaches his followers to break the bread and share the wine as often as possible. Moltmann argues that the community of the Church, as *ecclesia* and based on Christ, can bridge the gap between faith and lived experience.[6]

Jesus also teaches his disciples to share communion as often as possible. And why does he say this is important? "This is my body given for you; do this in remembrance of me."[7] In communal life, as *ecclesia*, the community shows the Being of God, and it becomes the manifest of the Risen Christ. In bridging the gap between faith and experience, the Church becomes a manifest of the Risen Christ.

But not only through the communal life should the Church manifest the Risen Christ. It should be a natural effect of life as a Christian to try, as well as possible, to follow in the footsteps of Christ and live out his example. Moltmann describes that all

---

4. Moltmann, 19.

5. Moltmann, 20.

6. Moltmann, 20–21.

7. Luke 22:19

Christians participate in "the kingly services of the Son of man and are witnesses of his liberating rule in their ecclesiastical life, as well as in their social one. The kingdom of all believers sets its stamp in the life of Christ's Church, both inward and outward."[8]

When the community of the Church exalts the crucified Jesus, then the Church becomes a manifest of the Risen Christ. It becomes a fellowship, not only with other humans but with God through Christ. Moltmann says, "In the fellowship of the Son of man it experiences the fulfillment of the promise of 'man.'"[9] The community experiences its liberation in the Church and through the Church when the community works for the liberation of the world. To Moltmann, being in fellowship with the "Son of Man" should affect the way one acts in the world so that the focus is to work to liberate all of creation. It creates a messianic character of the fellowship of the congregation, where we seek to continue the work of Christ.

Communion becomes an important symbol, as it should be a reminder of and a means to reinvigorate the messianic character of the fellowship. Moltmann puts it like this: "the assembled community should not merely give its worship the character of a messianic feast, but should also give its everyday individual and social functions the impress of messianic impulses."[10] Worship services should empower everyday life and everyday messianic impulses and, through communion, reconnect us to the Messiah, to Christ. For Moltmann, the assembled community is not just the communion of Christians, but more than that, it is also sent to the world. Therefore, the messianic fellowship should not huddle up in a Church building. The Sunday services were meant to send us out into the world as bearers of the messianic reality so that the

---

8. Moltmann, 108.

9. Moltmann, 108.

10. Moltmann, 262.

Church could be part of creating the new messianic age in local areas. In other words, it is the task of the Church to reconnect the world to Christ.

In Moltmann's ecclesiology, the Church is not centered around a congregation or building but around Christ. Where people faithfully follow and disciple Christ and act out his call to spread the gospel, that is where the Church is found. Moltmann argues that "we have to start from the event of Christ's presence to find the Church. In this sense, we start from the proposition: ubi Christus—ibi ecclesia."[11] This means that where Christ is, the Church is. This gets distorted if we start to see the Church as a building—a dead object—that cannot ever be truly present in the world. But the true Church, ecclesia, communion of the saints, etc., is not a finite happening but an infinite presence acted out in the lives of individuals.

Compared to the models Dulles presents, it is clear that Moltmann has a very active and Christ-centered focus. In some aspects, Moltmann could be placed in the Church as a herald because the focus is to proclaim the Gospel. This is what Christ sends his disciples out into the world to do: "Therefore go and make disciples of all nations, baptizing them in the name of the Father and of the Son and of the Holy Spirit, and teaching them to obey everything I have commanded you."[12] This is surely an aspect of discipling Christ. But for Moltmann, the ecclesiology ought to be an active community, not only proclaiming but actively seeking to establish the Kingdom of God here and now by following in the footsteps of Christ. As said, this is a more bottom-up approach than Dulles infers. It is clear that to Dulles, the Church is represented by the clergy, whereas Moltmann sees

---

11. Moltmann, 122.

12. Matt. 28:19-20

the Church as represented by the lived lives of the congregation. Dulles and Moltmann could probably agree on seeing the Church as the servant in Dulles's models. But again, this would be seen from opposite sides: Dulles looking top-down and Moltmann looking bottom-up.

So what is ecclesiology?

Dulles defines five models of the Church: The Church as Institution, Mystical Communion, Sacrament, Herald, and Servant. To put some perspective on Dulles's models, I drew on Moltmann, who defines his ecclesiology with a clear focus on discipling and how one should live as a follower of Christ. Moltmann's goal is to construct an ecclesiology from the bottom-up as opposed to Dulles's approach, which defines ecclesiology from the top-down. Combining these two different approaches, we are able to construct a well-rounded view of ecclesiology.

So, to round off this part, I will try to draw some general lines of what defines ecclesiology: As a fellowship in the presence of Christ, the Church is constituted by the faith and the presence of Christ in Christian communities. All Christians become carriers of the Church, continually bringing Christ into it's presence. Or, in a metaphor, each Christian is like a drop of water—a tiny part of the Church. Looking at a puddle, we can see it is just a combined work of many tiny drops. Again, an ocean is an even larger combined action by billions and billions of drops. One single drop hanging underneath a leaf after a rainfall does not, in itself, constitute a puddle or an ocean. It needs to gather with others to do so. But it is still an essential part of the entire ocean and will affect it.

Ecclesiology is not about defining the ocean but instead trying to define or frame how many tiny droplets can work together to create an ocean. In other words, ecclesiology is not defining structures but identifying Christlike patterns and actions in the lived lives, communities, and shared life.

This means that a well-rounded ecclesiology must draw strings to all of the other theological -ologies, as well as qualify how the Church chooses to lead and organize the community, value individuals as part of the community, and structure the gatherings and organization. In general, a well-rounded ecclesiology must describe how the Church intersects with the lived experience of the congregation and in what ways the congregations affect the Church.

Now, I will move on to the next part, where I will define ORT, and after that, try to condense ORE based on ORT and this introduction to ecclesiology.

PART TWO

Open and Relational Theology

The origins of Open and Relational Theology

Moving forward, we need to define ORT to gain an under-standing of the theological framework for our ecclesiology. First of all, I need to make a disclaimer: There are a variety of views on what ORT is. This is due to the fact that the term ORT was coined in the early 2000s by Oord in an effort to create an umbrella for many smaller theologies within the spectra of process thought, open theism, and relational theology.[1] Naturally, this creates a large diversity of voices within ORT. There is no single understanding of ORT. In this book, I can only introduce some of its nuances, and as I do, I'll stay as close as possible to Oord's definitions of ORT. When it makes sense, I will show the multi-tude of views on certain theological topics within ORT, but ulti-mately, I must choose an angle to show you the wonderful ideas of ORT. If you want to explore ORT deeper, I encourage you to do so. For that, the Center for Open and Relational Theology[2] is a goldmine.

But before we get too far into ORT, let's take a quick overview of the history behind this relatively new theological movement. Neglecting ancient theologians and thinkers, the ground for the

---

1. Oord, *Open and Relational Theology.*

2. C4ORT.com

contemporary movement was laid in 1929 when the English mathematician and philosopher Alfred North Whitehead published his collection of essays on cosmology called *Process and Reality*.[3] This publication lays the basis for Whitehead's *process philosophy*. The main book of Whitehead is that the universe is in an everlasting endeavor to incarnate itself. He writes, "Each creative act is the universe incarnating itself as one, and there is nothing above it by way of final condition."[4] This logic is also transposed unto God, the ultimate reality. God is in an everlasting process of experiencing the development of the entire creation moment by moment and co-creating this everlasting process together with the rest of creation.

Naturally, this quickly led to the development of process theology. Theologians like Charles Hartshorne and John Cobb quickly joined the stage with theological works building on Whitehead. Their main goal was to describe a view of God, in which God was not impassible and immutable but was affected by creation and temporal processes. If creation is an everlasting process then God would also have to be, as God experiences time moment by moment.

In 1980, the Seventh-day Adventist theologian Richard Rice published a book called *The Openness of God: The Relationship of Divine Foreknowledge and Human Free Will*.[5] Inspired by the ideas of process thought, Rice sought to argue for God being open to the future from a biblical viewpoint instead of through the lens of philosophy as process philosophy does. It is important here to note that even though open theism draws much inspiration from

---

3. Alfred North Whitehead, *Process and Reality: An Essay in Cosmology Gifford Lectures Delivered in the University of Edinburgh during the Session 1927-28*, Corr. ed (New York London: the Free press, 1978).

4. Whitehead.

5. Richard Rice, *The Openness of God: The Relationship of Divine Foreknowledge and Human Free Will*, Horizon (Nashville, TN: Review and Herald Pub. Association, 1980).

process theology, we cannot equate the two. Process theology and open theism differ on some very essential ideas, like how God interacts with the world, answers prayers, etc.[6] The exact nuances are not a topic I will discern here, as it is not entirely relevant to this book. For now, I will just note that open theism is inspired by process theology but does not equate to it.

The notion of God being open to the future of creation caught on when five theologians, including Richard Rice, *The Openness of God* in 1994.[7] This collection of five essays describing different aspects of open theism "borrowed" the title from Rice's book, and thus, the term open theism was born. The essays were written by Clark Pinnock, Richard Rice, John Sanders, William Hasker, and David Basinger, who each presented their view on a specific aspect of open theism.[8] These five thinkers largely constitute the "founders" of open theism.

Again, we touch on the difference between process theology and open theology. Process theology looks toward Whitehead for answers, and open theism looks toward the biblical narrative. Clark Pinnock writes, "Open theists are evangelicals who look to scripture, not to Whitehead. We object to the way process theology imposes a philosophical worldview—a kind of totalizing meta-narrative—on the Bible."[9] To put this another way, process thought is set within a frame of philosophy and is arguing from that point of view, whereas open theology is situated in the wisdom from the Jewish Rabbinic tradition up until the 1st century Rabbi, whom we acknowledge as the Messiah: Jesus Christ.

---

6. Clark H. Pinnock, ed., *The Openness of God: A Biblical Challenge to the Traditional Understanding of God* (Downers Grove, Ill: InterVarsity Press, 1994).

7. Pinnock.

8. Pinnock.

9. Clark H. Pinnock, *Most Moved Mover: A Theology of God's Openness.* (Place of publication not identified: WIPF & STOCK Publishers, 2019), 142.

To clarify, when Pinnock speaks of the philosophical view of God, he references the ideals of God as the most perfect entity: omnipotent, omniscient, omnipresent, omnibenevolent, impassible, and immutable. This view is seen in theologians like Anselm of Canterbury and Thomas Aquinas.[10]

Oord touches on somewhat the same point: "Process theology places priority on identifying a contemporary conceptuality. Open theology seeks for truth about reality in biblical metaphors and moves secondarily to philosophy."[11] It is not that open theology dismisses philosophy or Hellenistic influence, but it chooses to focus on the biblical narrative more than philosophy to seek the truth in the bible.

Oord came up with the term open and relational theology in the 2000s. His main goal is to make an umbrella for all the different variations of open theism. Some vary more toward process thought, and some vary more toward relational theology. Oord defines and expands these terms in many of his works. The following presentation of ORT in this book will be based mainly on Oord's work.

This chapter has laid out a little bit of the historical line, or the context, from which ORT arises. ORT chooses to place human freedom and divine love as the centerpiece of God's creation. From that, the whole theological scheme is developed: A God that so loved creation that God gave all of creation complete freedom to continue the creation process in their own spirit. That is the central anchor of ORT.

---

10. Pinnock, *MOST MOVED MOVER.*

11. Thomas Jay Oord, *The Nature of Love: A Theology* (St. Louis: Chalice Press, 2010), 90.

It all starts with Love

ORT starts with the notion that "God is Love."[1] Once again, ORT looks to the biblical narrative instead of the Hellenistic philosophy. The basis of the biblical narrative is that God, in essence, is love. God creates humans out of love, as seen in the Book of Genesis. God comes toward creation with open arms and even chooses to be incarnated into the world. In the Gospel of John, we read the famous line: "For God so loved the world that he gave his one and only Son, that whoever believes in him shall not perish but have eternal life."[2]

This is the sole pillar that ORT stands on: God is love and eternally loves creation. Oord starts with this proposition in his work *The Nature of Love: A Theology*, which in many ways, is his first articulation of ORT. In this book, Oord also concludes that "*God is Love*" has not been taken seriously by theologians through the ages: "One might conclude that love actually lies 'behind the curtain' of Christian theologies. Love is unseen and rarely mentioned, but love remains present, nonetheless. Perhaps this is true in some cases. But I believe love should take theology's center stage."[3] In ORT, Oord wants to place love at the center stage and

---

1. 1 John 4:8

2. John 3:16

3. Oord, 4.

works out his theological framework from the central notion that God is love.

Therefore, it is important to start this presentation on ORT by looking at how we can talk about love in a theological setting. It is important to understand on what ground most of ORT has been developed and from where the roots have grown. Defining love is, in itself, a great goal for a book. In *The Nature of Love,* Oord helps us by giving us a basic understanding of what love is. He writes, "To love is to act intentionally, in sympathetic/empathetic response to God and others, to promote overall well-being."[4] In 2022, Oord decided to update this definition to make it more accessible and fit better into the language of ORT: "To love is to act intentionally, in relational response to God and others, to promote overall well-being."[5]

This is the definition of love that I will work with for the time being. To Oord, this definition is valid whether we talk of divine or creaturely love. Love is purposefully enacted to create goodness, value, and beauty for overall well-being.

Oord emphasizes that love is not a feeling or a thing. Love is a verb; it is an action. It is just as John Mayer sings in his hit song neatly titled "Love is a Verb" from 2012: "Love is a verb / It ain't a thing / It's not something you own / It's not something you scream / When you show me love / I don't need your words."[6] Love is not a mere feeling of fondness but an active and powerful act in relational response to God and others to promote overall well-being. This is the footing of ORT.

To expand this a bit, I will run through each part of Oord's definition to expand on the concept of love. Diving into this

---

4. Oord, 17.

5. Thomas Jay Oord, *Pluriform Love: An Open and Relational Theology of Well-Being* (Sacra Sage Press, 2022), 28.

6. John Mayer, *Love Is a Verb*, Born and Raised (Columbia Records, 2012).

definition is easiest done if we start at the end and work our way backward. I will, therefore, begin with the last words of the definition.

7.1 … to promote overall well-being

The issue has often been to define the goal of love. What is the importance of love? Oord states that the goal of an active love is to promote well-being. This means that love creates good things like joy, happiness, and peace, all of which promote an overall sense of well-being.

Love aims to create overall well-being. This means your well-being, my well-being, and everyone's well-being will be enhanced. If I work for my own well-being separated from yours or the other way around, it will be a self-absorbed or self-neglecting act. This couldn't be labeled as loving because they only work one way. Love will always be an act that is beneficial to you and me. Love will always act to do good.

Oord says that "[l]ove wants flourishing to flourish."[7] Love is a generous act that lets both others and ourselves flourish. This is why the word "overall" becomes very important. All parts must grow and flourish for love to promote overall well-being.

A critique that often pops up concerning Oord's definition of love and promoting overall well-being is that it becomes very instrumentalized. This means that love becomes a mere tool for us creatures to work with. It becomes a tool by which we create overall well-being. I will not go into a further discussion about whether love should or should not be instrumentalized due to the limited scope of this book. For now, I will note that Oord's definition of

---

7. Oord, *Pluriform Love: An Open and Relational Theology of Well-Being*, 30.

love states that the goal is to create overall well-being and that this goal causes a critique of becoming too instrumentalized.

7.2   ... in relational response to God and others...

According to this definition, it takes two to love: one to act out love and one to receive. And more than that, it also involves God because God is love, as stated earlier. Oord says that "Entirely isolated individuals—if such even existed—could not love."[8] Love, as an act, presupposes a past relationship and actual real influences from each other prior to this moment. There is, so to speak, a need for a living relationship between two people for love to happen. There must be an emotional and empathetic connection between the two entities to be able to work intentionally in relational response for promoting overall well-being. One person must be able to feel with another and care for that other to act in love toward the other.

Love can flow between two individuals or internally in a larger group. It can be a flow between oneself and God. But the flow between two entities in a relationship is essential! This is contrary to our modern language, where we tend to overuse the word "love" or at least misuse it. We might say that we "love" a good cup of coffee when reading, though we are not in any relationship with the cup of coffee. There is no empathy between a person and the extract of ground beans. It would be more proper to say that we like good coffee when reading because it makes us feel well and creates a cozy atmosphere. But we do not really "love" it. There is no relational response between the coffee and us.

The interesting angle here is that God is not only is the source of love but essentially empowers creatures to love. God is

---

8. Oord, 33.

constantly calling creatures to act out of love toward each other. In this way, the calling to love is empowered by God and works in relational response to God and others around us. For love to be real, so to speak, there needs to be a relational response between oneself, God as the empowering cause and ground of love, and others.

7.3   To love is to act intentionally...

Love is an intentional act, not a passive feeling or emotion. As said earlier, love is a verb. Oord points to three major facets of acting intentionally: deliberation, motive, and freedom.[9]

Love is **deliberate** because we decide to love. We decide to act toward the promotion of well-being. It is often a spur-of-the-moment decision to love. We hug someone or call and talk to our lonely aunt. All of these are deliberate actions to show love.

Love has a **motive** because it purposely does well. An action meant to harm cannot be loving because it does not promote over-all well-being. We choose to act purposely to do good. However, we can sometimes mean to do good and end up harming someone else anyway. Sometimes, we try to act out of love with all the best intentions, but our efforts fail. We still act out of love, but evil can occur even though we have the best intentions.

Love needs us to be **free** actors in the world. If all my actions are predestined by a deity somewhere else, my love is not my action. An intentional action, which is predestined for me to do, is not built on my intentions. The intentionality lies on the shoulders of the one planning the action. To act intentionally demands the freedom to do so. Otherwise, it is not a deliberate and

---

9. Oord, 37.

purposeful effort to create overall well-being. Love only makes sense if we human beings are created to be free creatures.[10]

7.4 The love of God

Often, we talk about love as a mere emotion or desire, and for some, love is more devotion than anything else. But following this definition—that love is deliberate, has good motives, and is free—means that love is way more than this mere emotion. Love is an active force in our relationships and signifies the giving and receiving of influence. Oord says "[w]hile love requires relationality, it is more than relation alone."[11] Love means that we influence each other on a deeper level.

This becomes interesting when we look to combine the definition of love with a bit of proper theology. We must recognize that our love and God's love are analogous in the sense of actively working to promote overall well-being. God's love must share similarities with the creaturely love that we humans can express. Oord notes that "[w]e cannot follow Jesus' command to 'be merciful, just as your Father is merciful' (Lk. 6:36)[12] if bi-directional analogies do not exist between Creator and creatures."[13] We creatures are not able to follow these sorts of biblical commands if our love and God's love are not bi-directional analogous, meaning that creatures love in the same way as the Creator and vice versa.

In the First Epistle of John, it is made especially clear that God and creaturely love are analogous, as it says, "Whoever does

---

10. Oord, 37–38.
11. Oord, 44.
12. Quote from the New Revised Standard Version (NRSV)
13. Oord, *The Nature of Love*, 83.

not love does not know God, because God is love."[14] This quote is essential because it frames the directions of love. Oord says, "God is love's source, and God empowers creatures to respond."[15] When we love, God is the sole source of love, which empowers us to respond. Therefore, Oord also puts the notion of love being a relational response to God and others in his definition of love. Whenever we love, we are in relation with God, who is the source of all love.

God simply must love. Love is the essential attribute of God's eternal nature. I will explore this aspect further in Chapter 9: The Essence/Experience Binate. To phrase it differently, God cannot not love. It is not a possibility because God's very essence is love. When we creatures love, it is an occasional and contingent love. I choose from moment to moment to love because I am a temporary being. But God is eternal. And God's eternal essence *is* love. Oord emphasizes that "God could no more stop loving than stop existing. God's love is uncontrollable, not only in the sense that creatures cannot control divine love but also in the sense that God cannot stop loving."[16] God's essence is eternal love, and God, therefore, cannot stop loving. For now, we will leave this subject. Later in this book, I will pick up the subject again and elaborate on God's loving essence and changing experience in Chapter 9: The Essence/Experience Binate.

I write so much about love from the get-go because it is important to properly understand the coming presentation of ORT, which tries to frame ORT. The sole purpose of ORT is to create a fitting framework for a Christian theology of love. Because ORT considers love as God's primary attribute, it places God in a

---

14. 1 John 4:8

15. Oord, *Pluriform Love: An Open and Relational Theology of Well-Being*, 88.

16. Thomas Jay Oord, *The Uncontrolling Love of God: An Open and Relational Account of Providence* (Downers Grove, Illinois: InterVarsity Press, 2015), 161.

unique relational unity with creation. Oord notes, "As relational, God gives and receives with creatures and creation. Because love is relational, a theological framework that affirms a relational God makes sense of divine love."[17] Building on this, we shall look at God's responsive relation to creation in the coming chapter.

---

17. Oord, *Pluriform Love: An Open and Relational Theology of Well-Being*, 172.

God needs to be responsive to truly love

I n the previous chapter, we looked at how God is the sole source of love and empowering creatures to love. Given that love entails relationships, God participates in true give-and-take relationships with creation. God initiates this relationship with all of creation. Therefore, an important part of ORT is that God needs to be responsive to be relational.

A good example of God's relational side is seen in the story of Adam and Eve. After they have eaten the forbidden fruit, God comes to throw them out of Eden. But before that happens, God sits down in the grass and sows clothing of animal skin for Adam and Eve: "The Lord God made garments of skin for Adam and his wife and clothed them."[1] The story exemplifies how God did not just chuck Adam and Eve out of the garden but took the time to slaughter an animal, tan and prepare the skin, and then sow clothes for them to wear. This is a deeply loving, empathetic, and relational response to Adam and Eve's misdeed. This action shows that God does not just turn away when creatures overstep their boundaries. Instead, God keeps on loving and keeps being empathetic. God responds to the situation and works to squeeze

---

1. Gen. 3:21

every last bit of goodness out of the evil that happens. It shows a compassionate, loving God that always loves first.

Because God first loved creation, creation is made able to love. God loved first and is the source of all love. God does not control human beings but instead gives them freedom to choose whether to love or not. When we love, we freely choose to accept God's invitation and love in response to divine empowerment. This means that creation is more than a mere channel through which God can act out love. As Oord puts it, "They [humans] are more than mere tubes or channels through which God works. They have real agency and intrinsic value. Humans should love themselves, in the sense of acting to promote their own well-being."[2] Creatures have a true free agency to choose whether or not to respond to God's invitation. God will always and eternally invite us into love. But we choose whether to accept or decline the invitation.

8.1 Panentheism

The relationship between Creator and creation springs from the special bond between the two. God is immanent in all of creation, meaning God is present in every bit of matter in the universe. Many ORT thinkers would support a panentheistic view, meaning that all of creation is within God. This does not mean that everything *is* God (that view is known as pantheism); panentheism means that the entire creation is located *in* God. This creates a very close relationship between God and creation while keeping the essential separate distinctions of the Creator and the created. God created us in God's image, but not as God.

Clark Pinnock, who is one of the founding fathers of open theism, posits the idea that God not only created the universe

---

2. Oord, 90.

but still calls forth new life, new ideas, and new creations. God always works to renew the world and is the source of all creative action. "God is on the inside of creation, in the processes not in the gaps," Pinnock writes and continues, "God is immanent throughout the universe in all of its changeableness and contingency and active in the whole long process of its development. The Creator has a mysterious relationship with every bit of matter and with every person."[3] ORT sets out to recover this sense of God's immanence. When we take part in creating, we are taking part in the very being of God. Our relationship with God is constituted in this creative action, and God constantly seeks for us to take part in this relationship.

That ORT argues for panentheism means that all of creation becomes endlessly valuable, as all of creation carries with it the image of the Divine. God is present in all and everything, and therefore, all and everything should be treated as endlessly valuable.

8.2 The affected God

ORT argues that we see an affected, mutable, and responsive God in scripture. God shows many feelings: compassion, anger, sadness, joy, etc., feelings that build on God showing divine emotions in relational response to creatures. We see a God who can love! This is important because only relational beings with emotions are able to love. As Oord writes, "Love requires experiencing others, in the sense of affecting and affected. Love responds. Lovers often also experience emotions in relation to what occurs. Without emotional experiences, God could not feel empathy, joy, or sadness and express love in response."[4] ORT argues that God has emo-

---

3. Pinnock, *The Openness of God*, 112–13.

4. Oord, *Pluriform Love: An Open and Relational Theology of Well-Being*, 123.

tions to respond to creation through relationships. Throughout scripture, this is shown in a multitude of divine emotions.

That God actively seeks a relationship with all of creation is an important feature of Christianity. For Pinnock, this is the great narrative of the Bible: that a triune personal God seeks relationships of love and affection with creation. He calls this a "revelation of unheard of relatedness and intimacy."[5] This relationship also indicates a need for God to be able to change instead of being immutable. For the give-and-receive relationship with God to exist, God needs to be susceptible to influence from creation and able to change based on the influence. This view of God is seen many times in the biblical narrative. Here, we see a compassionate God who is influenced by creatures. A quick example of this would be Hezekiah pleading to God for more years to live and God succumbing to this plea, changing the planned action and letting Hezekiah live on. Afterwards, Hezekiah strikes this deal again and keeps arguing with God.[6]

Pinnock interestingly uses God's responsiveness to point out the peculiarity of open theism as opposed to the more classic views of God. Pinnock notes that the understanding of God as impassible stems more from Plato and the Hellenistic inspiration of much classical theology than from the biblical narrative.[7] In scripture, God is not a stoic, cool, and collected individual. God is emotional, involved, and vulnerable. An example can be drawn from the book of Hosea. God speaks, "My heart recoils within me, my compassion grows warm and tender."[8] Or from Genesis, where God regrets creating humans: "And the Lord was sorry that he had made humans on the earth, and it grieved him to his

---

5. Pinnock, *MOST MOVED MOVER*, 28.

6. 2 Kings 20:1-11

7. Pinnock, *The Openness of God*, 118.

8. Hosea 11:8 (RSV).

heart."[9] God is not a distant, impassible God. God is responsive, suffering, and grieving. As well, we often see God rejoicing or being pleased. Pinnock makes the point that God chooses to really suffer by being open to the world: "God does not just imagine what it would be like to suffer, [God] actually suffers because of [God's] decision to love. God has chosen to be open to the world and to share in its suffering because of [God's] love."[10] God is then not this impassible being. God knows suffering, loss, and grief. Pinnock argues that if God did not know and experience these emotions, God would not be able to be in real relationships with human beings.

God's transcendence over the world does not prevent interaction with or affection for the world. ORT says that God transcends the world but is not distant from the world. God wants, and more than that needs, relationships with creation. This need for a relationship is inherent in a triune God. The trinity itself points to a relational ontology: a living relational dimension to the Divine.

In no way can God be viewed as a self-sufficient, headstrong ruler. As Pinnock puts it, "God exists as diverse persons united in a communion of love and freedom. God is the perfection of love and communion, the very antithesis of self-sufficiency."[11] ORT argues that God's inherent relatability is shown through the Holy Trinity, where not even God is only One but a divine unity in a living relationship.

God is the antithesis of self-sufficiency. God needs creaturely relationships to keep the creative process moving forward. ORT affirms that God has not distanced Godself but seeks to keep the creative process moving. For that, God needs creaturely responses.

---

9. Gen. 6:6 (NRSV).

10. Pinnock, 118–19.

11. Pinnock, 108.

8.3 God is repenting

So, God is affected, and God experiences changes. This is also seen in scripture, where God often repents and changes plans or direction. The scripture shows us a God who is not a perfectly unchangeable being but actually repents, alters a decision, or bargains with creatures.

Many times, biblical writers say that God repents. Oord states it appears more than forty times.[12],[13] When God repents, it does not mean that God turns away from sin, but that God is sorrowed by the outcome of a situation, has a change of mind, and wishes to alter an earlier plan or action. We see that God plans to do one thing but then has a change of mind due to creaturely prayer or action. Oord says, "A timeless God can't alter course, but a Living God can. Scripture passages saying God chooses mercy, responds to needs and liberates the oppressed make little sense if God is timeless."[14] Because God is open to the future and has not pre-settled every action, God can repent. Furthermore, our actions and prayers make sense. For the timeless God, creatures are mere robots. For the living and dynamic God, creatures are relational beings to interact with, influence, and be influenced by.

The American theologian and pastor Gregory Boyd argues that this notion of divine perfection, meaning an immutable, impassible, unchangeable God that will never repent or so alike, is a relic from Hellenistic culture and philosophy, which has shaped our Western mentality. Boyd especially points out that Plato's

---

12. I have not been able to confirm this number, but from different encyclopedias and bible commentaries, it was easy to locate more than twenty verses where God repents. So, over forty times seems quite plausible. I found: Gen 6:6, Gen 6:7, Ex 32:12-14, Deut 32:36, Judg 2:18, 1 Sam 15:11, 1 Sam 15:35, 2 Sam 24:16; 1 Chron 21:15; Psa 90:13, Psa 106:45, Psa 135:14, Jer 18:8, Jer 26:3, 13, 19, Jer 42:10, Joel 2:13-14; Amos 7:3, 6; Jonah 3:9-10; 4:2

13. Oord, *Open and Relational Theology*, 31.

14. Oord, 31.

notions of divine perfection and timelessness are to blame here[15] and argues that the motif of divine openness is truer from a biblical viewpoint. To Boyd, it is important to make an effort to show that the Christian tradition should not keep building on the remnants of Hellenistic culture but should stand more firmly on the Jewish legacy.

Oord also argues that it is extremely difficult to fit the biblical notions of God into a philosophy of divine timelessness and unchangeability. When we look to scripture, we see a God that is giving and receiving in relationship with creatures. We see a God that is changing, repenting, and mourning. We do not encounter a God that is timeless and completely perfect. Oord notes that "[i]nteraction, by nature, requires a time dimension. Each moment of an interactive love relationship has a before and after. Interactive relationships change the experience of those in relation. Love requires that lovers change."[16] God would not be able to interact and relate with creation if God was not affected by time and had the ability to change. An interaction demands a time before and a time after the given event. ORT argues that God must exist moment by moment together with the rest of creation to experience and partake in real relationships.

In this way, ORT takes a stand against the Thomistic legacy, which says God is an immovable mover which cannot have real relationships with creation, and the Calvinistic legacy, which says God is a solo performer with no need for a creaturely agency. These ideas are quite widespread in modern times, but as Pinnock argues in his suitably named book *The Most Moved Mover*, "If [God] is pure actuality, impassive, and timeless, or if the entire future is settled already, the basis of the significance of our lives

---

15. Gregory A. Boyd, *God of the Possible: A Biblical Introduction to the Open View of God* (Grand Rapids, Mich: Baker Books, 2000), 115.

16. Oord, *The Nature of Love*, 78.

is undercut."[17] ORT argues that our being and lives make sense because we have a real significance, both to the rest of creation and to God. If we took Thomism or Calvinism seriously, the significance of our lives would be undercut, and we would be mere pawns in a universal chess game that we do not play ourselves.

Boyd takes a similar approach to this. He argues that classic theism cannot accept that God should be open and relational because it looks to place God in a box of philosophical preconceptions, namely that the Divine is timeless, immutable, and impassible. Boyd draws forth the essence/experience binate and notes that while God's essence can remain the same through all of the ages, God's experience and knowledge must change. If not, then God's knowledge of the future is unchanging, and then the future must be unchangeable. Boyd writes, "On the other hand, if we simply accept the plain meaning of Scripture, we learn that God sometimes regrets how decisions [God has] made turn out. [God] sometimes question how aspects of the future will go."[18] As shown earlier, God often repents or regrets something that has happened or changes the plans for future actions. ORT argues that we also see a God that is changing mid-action due to creaturely actions. In that sense, God can question the future and can choose to alter it together with creation.

Two examples of God repenting that are often drawn forth by open and relational thinkers are the stories of Jonah and King Hezekiah.

Fistly, we have the story of Jonah, whom God tells to go to Nineveh and preach to them so they will turn from their evil ways. At first, Jonah runs away, and we have the "big fish" incident. Jonah finally arrives and preaches. Then, the Ninevites repent, and God "saw what they did and how they turned from their evil

---

17. Pinnock, *MOST MOVED MOVER*, 158.

18. Boyd, *God of the Possible*, 86–87.

ways, he relented and did not bring on them the destruction he had threatened."[19] God changes plans due to creaturely actions. This does not go down well with Jonah, who is angry about why he needed to take that entire journey just for God to show mercy. God tells Jonah off for being more interested in seeing their destruction than redemption: "should I not have concern for the great city of Nineveh, in which there are more than a hundred and twenty thousand people who cannot tell their right hand from their left."[20]

The story shows a God who truly cares for creation and wants to be in relationships with creatures. Nineveh has shut out God, turned its back on God, and does not want the relationship. Jonah goes to open up this relationship to show God wants to draw them close again and make the Ninevites turn to God again. Jonah's task was not to proclaim the destruction of Nineveh but to open the Ninevites to a new relationship with God. And we see a God that relents on the destruction, changes the plans, and truly cares about creatures.

Secondly, we find a great example of God repenting in 2 Kings 20, where Hezekiah falls ill. Isaiah comes to him and tells him that he surely will perish soon and needs to get his house ready for his passing away. Hezekiah is distraught, pleads, and begs God to let him live on: "I beg You, O Lord, remember how I have walked before You in truth and with a whole heart. I have done what is good in Your eyes."[21] Even before Isaiah reaches the exit of the room, God comes to him and tells him that the plans have changed. Isaiah says to Hezekiah, "This is what the Lord, the God of your father David, says, "I have heard your prayer. I have seen your tears. See, I will heal you. On the third day, you must go up

---

19. Jonah 3:10

20. Jonah 4:11

21. 2. Kings 20:3

to the house of the Lord. And I will add fifteen years to your life."[22] God changes the plan after Hezekiah pleads for his life. Hezekiah does not change his ways but simply lets God remember the good he has done, praying and supplying God with information. That is enough to make God repent and let Hezekiah live on.

A critique of the ORT interpretation of the story of Jonah and Nineveh could be that it seems God never planned to destroy the city but knew that a threat that big would make the Ninevites repent and change their wicked ways. It may seem like a weird plan, but it sure did work. The pure threat of being obliterated made the Ninevites repent. ORT uses the story of Hezekiah to show God purely repenting and argues this same thing happened in the story of Jonah. Hezekiah does not change, but God does. ORT, therefore, infers that the same happens in the story of Nineveh. God sees the change in the people, repents, and does not destroy the city. This is a pattern seen in many stories of the Old Testament.

God's repentance stresses God's willing activity in the world. ORT argues that God seeks to be generous, sensitive, vulnerable, relational, and loving more than being in control and having all the power. Pinnock notes that "[i]t allows us to think of God as taking risks. Instead of locating God above and beyond history, it stresses God's activity in history, responding to events as they happen, in order to accomplish [God's] purposes."[23] ORT allows us to encounter God as a responsive risk-taker. God is willing to give us a chance to prove ourselves, repent, and make the right decisions. God gives up some power for us to gain the power of free will and agency. This demands that God can repent, experience, be relational, and change paths without giving up God's essence.

---

22. 2. Kings 20:5-6

23. Pinnock, *The Openness of God*, 125.

The story of Hezekiah is also important for ORT's argument on why prayer makes sense. If God could not change and certainly knew the future, then why should we pray? Firstly, we pray for God to truly make a change. If we believe that God only wants good and only has plans for our good, then why pray for God to change that? Then all situations, whether they feel good or bad, must be good. Secondly, if God already foreknows all that happens and cannot alter these plans, then there are no live options. Why pray then? Our future is settled whether we pray or not. More than that, God has preplanned when, where, and for what we will pray; it is not even our own prayer or decision. Oord argues that while these views are not motivating one to pray, the views of ORT will be motivating: "What I say makes a difference to God and creation. The future is still in the making, and my efforts influence others and God. What I do matters. [...] prayer affects the one praying, those prayed for, and the God who responds. An open future is different because we prayed."[24] ORT argues that our prayer matters exactly because God is open and can repent and change. That means that my prayer will influence and affect how tomorrow turns out.

Holtzen moves ORT forward in this aspect, as he argues that God not only gives power to creation but also trusts us and believes in us to do what is right. God gives creation free agency, installs in creation the power of love, and keeps calling and luring creation to act from love. From that point on, God trusts creation to keep creation going. God trusts creation to be God's co-creating partners. Holtzen writes, "God as being of maximal love and we, cocreators in whom God has chosen to share power with, leads me to conclude that God actually believes in us [and]

---

24. Oord, *Open and Relational Theology*, 43.

because God is a being of maximum love, God seeks a way to trust us, not more than that, love leads God to believe in us."[25]

God trusts us creatures and believes in us to do the right thing, to take care of creation in our role as co-creators. But if God can trust and believe in us, then God must be able to doubt us and lose confidence. Holtzen agrees and points out that "God may have real doubts about our future choices based on our past and present choices and intentions."[26] Exactly because the future is open, we are free to act as we want to and make whatever choices we want, whether it is working to cooperate with God or not. God must actually and truly trust in us to do what is right. On top of this, God can inspire, lure, and help us along the right path. But for trust and belief to be real, it must leave God open to having real doubts about us and our choices. ORT argues that God has real doubts about us, just as much as God believes in us.

In the same sense, ORT argues that God cannot exist "risk-free." When the future is open, and creatures have free agency, God risks that God's plans will be foiled, as well as risk being rejected by creation. This is the risk that follows when entering into a relationship of mutual trust with an autonomous being. Holtzen argues that "[t]rust, then, is a risk even for the divine. If God desires cooperation, then God cannot exist risk free. Even God cannot have the proverbial cake and eat it too. To be a God of love is to be a God of trust."[27] God cannot exist risk-free, because God wishes to be in real relationships with creation. ORT argues that just as much as creation hopes for God to proactively work for the good of all creatures, God hopes for all creatures to cooperate in God's work.

---

25. William Curtis Holtzen, *The God Who Trusts: A Relational Theology of Divine Faith, Hope, and Love* (Westmont: InterVarsity Press, 2019), 107–9.

26. Holtzen, 121.

27. Holtzen, 133.

ORT argues that God's risk will always be the wisest of all possible risks. God's omniscience makes everything possibly knowable present in God's mind. Therefore, God can keep adjusting plans and hopes for the future due to what the situation is like at the present moment. Omniscience means that God can always make the wisest possible choice and take the wisest possible risk.

Gregory Boyd also notes that "God's risks are always wise, of course, for the possibility of things going God's way is worth it. But they are risks nonetheless. In a cosmos populated by free agents, the outcome of things—even divine decisions—is often uncertain."[28] God takes the risk that plans may fail due to creatures not cooperating. This risk is why God needs to be able to change and even repent. When plans fail due to creatures not cooperating, then God must be able to lay new plans and start luring creations toward them. The future is open, and so is God's planning—open to the risk of being in real relationships and therefore not able to control the outcome of creatures' free agency. ORT argues that sometimes God may even plan for something that goes wrong. Then, God must repent and change lanes to move forward again. Repentance and change happen in God's experience, while God's essence of everlasting love always remains.

---

28. Boyd, *God of the Possible*, 58.

The Essence/Experience Binate

According to ORT, God is an emotional, responsive, and passible being that will change over time. At this point, many will raise an important critique: Can we then actually trust God? As in, could God throw a temper tantrum or have a moral meltdown due to creaturely disobedience and choose to smite Earth? Or could God choose to live a great distance from Earth and never interact with creation again? How can we trust God if God could all of a sudden change to be unloving and hateful? This is a serious critique that ORT thinkers have taken into account and given significant attention to. To answer these questions and critiques, ORT thinkers argue for an essence/experience binate: that God has an everlasting essence—love—which God cannot turn away from, and that God has an experiential dimension, which changes as God acquires new knowledge of creation and experiences emotions.

First of all, let us look at God's essence. Earlier, I stated that ORT starts with the notion that "God is love."[1] When we talk about the essence/experience binate, ORT states that God's essence is love. Love is not a mere attribute among other characteristics of equal importance in the divine being. God *is* love. The American anthropologist and theologian Gabriel Gordon notes

---

1. 1 John 4:8

that God's essence is love "to such an extent that you could replace the term God with Love and you would be saying the same thing."[2] This is again building on 1 John 4:8, which carries the notion that the very essence of God is pure love and vice versa. When we see true love, we see God's essence. This also relates to the panentheistic view. God is present as love in all of creation.

The important point for ORT is that God's essence remains unchanging and everlasting, while God's experience may change. This anchors God so that God can experience emotions without those leading to a moral meltdown. Oord states that "God relates intimately with creation and feels all that's publicly feelable. But God's emotions never lead to evil. Because the divine character never changes."[3] God's emotions can never lead to God doing evil because God's essence is eternally loving, and love enhances the overall well-being contrary to evil. This also implies that there are things God cannot do. God is limited in actions by the essence that is love. I will touch more on this in the coming Chapter 11: Amipotence, but for now, I will not examine this divine self-limitation further.

God becomes consistently dependable precisely because God's essence is unchanging. We know we can always trust God because God's essence will always be love. From this essence of love, God can respond to creation, experience, and be emotional. God responds to the changing needs of creation and will, therefore, be able to change directions when necessary. This change in experience does not violate the integrity of God's essence. Pinnock explains it like this: "God is changeless in nature, but his nature is that of a creative person who interacts. God's immutability does not rule out God's responsiveness, the quality that enables God to deal with every new happening and to bend it toward [God's]

---

2. Gabriel Gordon, *God Speaks: A Participatory Theology of Biblical Inspiration*, 2021, 91.

3. Oord, *Open and Relational Theology*, 58.

objectives without violating its integrity."[4] God becomes able to respond through being affected and experiencing time and creation. But God still has an immutable essence, and that is love. The essence is everlasting and unchanging, but the experience changes over time.

The essence/experience binate can be seen as a rock. Put the rock in a lake; it will be wet, but it is still a rock. Or place it on the forest floor; it might be covered in moss, but it is still a rock. Place it in the sun. It will be hot, but it is still a rock. God's essence is like the rock: unchanging, everlasting love. God's experience is the different biomes that the rock might be placed in. It might be wet, hot, or covered in moss. This is changeable, but it will not change the essence of the rock.

In short, God can only function as God, meaning that God can only act in accordance with God's essence. God would not be able to act out of evil or hate, as God's essence is love. Gordon nicely phrases this: "God can do all things which accord to God's nature. In other words, God can only act as God. All-powerful means that God can do all things that are within God's nature and that God is not limited from being fully God."[5] If the action does not fit into God's perfect nature or essence, God cannot perform that action. God's omnipotence is inherently limited by God's essence—love.

Exactly because God cannot act against the nature or essence of God, we can trust God. God is not this unstable toddler who acts randomly based on on-the-fly inputs and emotions. God has a grounded, eternally unchanging essence. This essence remains the same, but God's experience evolves moment by moment. Oord argues that this divine experience, flexible and forming, is like the growing universe. It changes and evolves, not in gigantic

---

4. Pinnock, *The Openness of God*, 118.

5. Gordon, *God Speaks*, 27.

shifts, but in small incremental experiences. This makes God unchanging in one aspect—essence—but changing in another—experience,[6] ergo the essence/experience binate.

To sum up the essence/experience binate in one paragraph, ORT argues that God will always work to truly love all of creation. The ways God expresses this love depend on what's best at any given moment. To evaluate what is best, God must learn and experience moment by moment to evaluate options and choose a path to follow. The essence is love—forever unchanging, expressed in the best way possible, adapted and changed according to experience.

Oord states that "God assesses how to help us and acts accordingly in each instance."[7] Yet through all these changes, God's steadfast love never ceases. As it says in Lamentations, "The steadfast love of the Lord never ceases, his mercies never come to an end; they are new every morning."[8] ORT argues that God's love will never cease. God's love and mercy are replenished each morning and can never be changed. Yet God experiences the same way creation does and can, from that experience, change paths and plans.

---

6. Oord, *Open and Relational Theology*, 39.

7. Oord, 41.

8. Lam. 3:22-23 (RSV).

Creation and freedom

We have looked at how ORT argues that God is love and how God is ever responding to the universe and even repents. This responsiveness leads to the idea of the essence/experience binate: how God has a steadfast loving essence and a changing experience of creation and how to respond to creation. Now, we turn to another element of God's responsiveness. ORT argues that humans are created with ultimate freedom. This means that God cannot coerce or physically alter creation because it would overwrite creaturely freedom. This is a main pillar of open theism but also one that ORT embraces as essential and builds on. Therefore, I will draw in material from different open theists to cast some light on the topic of creaturely freedom.

To begin with, I want to be clear on some terms. When we talk about coercing in ORT, we do not talk of psychological, violent, or bodily coercing but metaphysical coercing.

To elaborate, let us look at how Oord qualifies metaphysical coercion. Some see **coercion in a psychological sense**. I could use threats or emotional pressure to deprive you of your freedom. You could choose whether to yield to my coercion or not and thereby reap the consequences. In this sense, I do not take complete control of you. You have your free will to yield or not. Psychologically, I could coerce you into my ways. Or I could use **violent coercion** and act in ways of conflict: war, domestic altercations, terror, etc. Violent coercion involves localized bodies or objects that wreak destruction. My violent coercion will make you change your ways out of fear for your safety and well-being. Lastly, I could act out **bodily coercion**. I could grab you before you walked in front of a bus or push you out in front of it, depending on my mood and wishes. I use my localized body to change the ways of your localized body. Bodily coercion is simply using my muscles against yours.[1]

When talking of divine coercion, we should not think of psychological, violent, or bodily coercion because they are only creaturely available. God, meanwhile, has no localized body and cannot be violent or use bodily or psychological coercion. When we are talking of divine coercion, we must think of **metaphysical coercion**. This means to control entirely, removing free will to replace it with God's own will. Oord defines metaphysical coercion as involving "unilateral determination, in which the one coerced loses all capacity for causation, self-organization, agency or free will. To coerce in this metaphysical sense is to act as a sufficient cause, thereby wholly controlling the other or the situation."[2] For God to coerce creatures, we need to think of this complete control, where God alone decides how a human should move and act. For God to coerce, in a metaphysical sense, God would control humans entirely as if we were remote-controlled robots.

ORT argues that God *does not* coerce humans because God loves creation and creatures and wants a true relationship, which can only happen with free individuals. God cannot control us but only sets us free instead, letting go of control. God has given the ultimate freedom to creatures. Love is not possible in a coerced setting. You cannot coerce someone into truly loving you. Because God truly wants our love and relationships, God has

---

1. Oord, *The Uncontrolling Love of God*, 182.
2. Oord, 183.

given us complete freedom, without coercion, to either choose to love God or not. Pinnock points out "God can have our love only if we decide to give it [...] God empowers but does not overpower."[3] ORT argues that it is up to us whether or not we want to give God our love or not. We need to want to love God for the love to be real. God works through empowering rather than overpowering. We draw on God's essence when we love. God empowers us to love instead of controlling our actions.

This is phrased a bit differently by the open theist John Sanders. He states that "love does not force its own way on the beloved."[4] We are empowered by God, but not coerced into loving. I have my own free will and can choose to love God and others or not. I can even choose to hate them if that is what I want.

Oord uses the revelation of God that we have in Jesus Christ to show God's noncoercive call to love and deny divine coercion. Looking at the stories of Jesus, we see that he did not coerce but always called, inspired, and motivated. In the Gospel of Matthew, Jesus calls his disciples to "follow me."[5] The disciples choose for themselves. They are called and choose a response to this call. The way Jesus calls mirrors the way God calls us to follow, and then God awaits. Oord then notes, "God's call awaits our free response. Jesus lovingly gives of himself, calls upon others to respond in freedom, and does good to all."[6] We are lovingly called and must respond by either acting out of love or turning our backs on the call.

The American open and relational theologian Mark Karris makes an interesting comparison between humans and robots.

---

3. Clark H. Pinnock, *Flame of Love: A Theology of the Holy Spirit* (Downers Grove, Ill: InterVarsity Press, 1996), 157.

4. John Sanders, *The God Who Risks: A Theology of Divine Providence*, 2nd ed., Rev. ed (Downers Grove, Ill: IVP Academic, 2007), 193.

5. Mt. 4:19

6. Oord, *The Nature of Love*, 129.

Had God created robots, then God could control them either way God wanted to. But God created free individual human beings. Karris says, "Since we are not robots and God's nature is love, there are some things God cannot do. God does not override our free will, therefore [God] cannot single-handedly control people. Instead, [God] lovingly draws people to [God'self] and waits patiently for us to embrace [the] graceful invitation."[7] God must call, lure, draw, and invite us. But God cannot go further. This divine self-limitation is an important point in ORT. Without divine self-limitation, humans could not be free. God invites, insists, and calls. Creation responds freely. The thing here is that God has not chosen to self-limit, as in God cannot choose not to be limited anymore. God's essence, love, is the limiting factor, and God cannot turn away from this, as "God is love." It would not be loving to coerce creation and remove freedom.

Pinnock adds to this argument by pulling forth the biblical image of the Church as the bride of God: "For the wedding of the Lamb has come, and his bride has made herself ready."[8] From this, Pinnock argues that "God created the world out of love and with the goal of acquiring a people who would, like the bride, freely participate in [God's] love [and God] values freedom, not so much as an end in itself, but as an instrument to make possible what [God] really longs for, love. God gives us real freedom because of [God's] desire for loving relationships."[9] God longs for truly loving relationships and to have real intimacy with all of creation. This could not be done with robots. Loving relationships are built on freedom. We choose to be part of this relationship

---

7. Mark Gregory Karris, *Divine Echoes: Reconciling Prayer with the Uncontrolling Love of God*, 2018, 58.

8. Rev.19:7

9. Pinnock, *MOST MOVED MOVER*, 126.

and love God. We make this choice every day, as we also do with our spouses, friends, and family.

Sanders also adds another aspect. The freedom that God has granted is also the freedom to be creative and participate in this project, which is creation. We are free to keep up creating creation, so to speak. "God grants humans genuine freedom to participate in this project, and [God] does not force them to comply."[10] Creativity is not possible in a coerced environment without free will. Or at least it would not be one's own creation, but a creation done by the one controlling. To be truly creative, we must be truly free. God wants us to take care of creation, to be part of the co-creation process, and that stresses the need for creaturely freedom.

But no matter how we choose to respond, love is continually poured into creation. The American process theologian and scholar C. Robert Mesle argues that this love is the very foundation of freedom and life within all creatures. It is up to us creatures to choose a response to this love. "This gracious—unmerited—love is continually poured into all creation. The choice lies with us on how we will respond. We have the power to accept or reject that love and the call it involves."[11] Love is the calling from God to all of creation. When we choose to love, we follow God's call. But then what when we choose not to love?

10.1 Attunement

Choosing not to respond to God's invitation and call to love equivalates to turning our back on God—to estrange ourselves from the very essence of God. ORT would define not responding

10. Sanders, *The God Who Risks*, 174.

11. C. Robert Mesle, *Process Theology: A Basic Introduction* (St. Louis, Mo: Chalice Press, 1993), 39.

to God as sinning. In this sense, sinning simply becomes choosing not to respond to God's call and instead taking actions and choices that estrange us from God or that counteract God. Oord argues that we humans always are the source of estrangement. God would never seek to estrange creatures from the Creator. Oord writes, "God's mind doesn't need to be changed about us. God's mind is set: God will always relate with and love us. That's guaranteed. We need to change our minds (and actions) about God. And about ourselves and others."[12] Humans need to attune themselves to God. Humans need to change their minds and actions to follow the call and lure from God. God will eternally love creation, but the question is whether humans will accept that call or not. Will humans attune themselves to God?

So, ORT argues that sin is estranging ourselves from God. From that, it follows that atonement is all about attunement to God's being. Oord argues that atonement in ORT is not focused on transactions (like penal substitution) but instead on transformations. It is not about paying a debt but rather about attuning to one's life and following God's call to love. God would rather have people attuned to God's being so they start becoming consistent lovers than an abstract price to be paid for atoning. That means that atonement is not about meeting specific legal requirements and paying a specific price but instead transforming one's life to follow the call of God and, through that, promote genuine flourishing for oneself and others. And God invites all into this loving relationship and attuning. Oord argues that "[n]o one is irredeemable. God also cares about saving animals and creation because God loves everyone and everything. Atonement involves attunement: attuning to God's love and responding accordingly."[13] ORT becomes more holistic here. God's grace and redemption

---

12. Oord, *Open and Relational Theology*, 109.

13. Oord, 106.

are for all of creation, not just mankind. Man is atoned by attuning to God and living life according to this attunement.

Therefore, salvation in the view of ORT is to accept the invitation given by the amazing love of God and attune to this love. ORT argues that God's love and the invitation to attune are always at hand. We choose whether to accept or decline this invitation. God calls and lures us toward the invitation, but we are free humans, and we can choose to ignore this invitation and ignore the atonement. If we do, we will naturally suffer consequences. These consequences are not damnation or penalty from the divine being, but natural consequences that follow from saying "No" to the positive power of love. Oord says that "[w]e don't get a divine spanking, nor are we annihilated. God always invites, calls, and woos us toward well-being. God's love never gives up and always hopes."[14] These views lean toward a more universalistic notion of atonement but do not go all the way to universal reconciliation since we still have the freedom to decline God.

10.2   Evil arises from non-attuned beings

The fact that we can choose to decline the positive, good power of the love of God also helps explain how evil arises. All creatures have genuine free will to either attune to God or not. Free will also makes it possible to misuse our freedom or agency and choose to act out evil. ORT argues that sinning is acting against the love of God, meaning that sin, evil, tragedy, and so on are undermining rather than promoting overall well-being. God does not allow this or enforce evil as some sort of divine punishment or as part of a greater plan. Evils are, in essence, non-God. Evil happens when creatures rebel or act contrary to God, who is pure

---

14. Oord, 113.

love. God has created creatures ultimately free so that all could be in a true relationship with God. This is a freedom that demands responsibility on the part of humans. If we are not responsible, then we can wind up misusing our freedom to do evil and harm. Oord argues that this means we cannot rightly blame God for permitting evil since it is done by free creatures. Oord writes, "The God whose loving nature necessarily gives freedom/agency to creatures cannot withhold, withdraw, or override the gifts God gives. We cannot rightly blame this God for permitting genuine evil."[15] God cannot override the gift of freedom, as discussed in Chapter 10: Creation and Freedom. Therefore, God cannot single-handedly stop a school shooter, drunk driver, robber, liar, adulterer, or any other act of evil.

It then raises the question: Given our inability to manage free will and the potential of evil, why then did God give us free will? Is that not, in some way, permitting evil?

The well-known writer and Anglican lay theologian C.S. Lewis has also addressed this. Though he is not an explicit open theologian, the following quote has been adopted into ORT and cited by many thinkers because it so accurately frames this question:

Why, then, did God give them free will? Because free will, though it makes evil possible, is also the only thing that makes possible any love or goodness or joy worth having. A world of automata—of creatures that worked like machines—would hardly be worth creating. The happiness which God designs for [God's] higher creatures is the happiness of being freely, voluntarily united to [God] and to each other in an ecstasy of love between a man and a woman on this earth is mere milk and water. And for that they must be free.[16]

---

15. Oord, *The Nature of Love*, 126.

16. C. S. Lewis, *Mere Christianity*, überarbeitete und erweiterte Auflage, mit neuer Einleitung der drei Bücher 'Broadcast Talks', 'Christian Behaviour' und 'Beyond Personality', C. S. Lewis Signature Classics Edition (London: HarperCollins, 2016), 48.

Lewis states that were we not created to be free, we would all be *creatio automata*—basically, advanced robots that could be programmed to do whatever the controlling part wants. ORT argues this is not what God wants. When we read the story of Adam and Eve in the Garden of Eden, we read that God created humans free to be in a truly loving relationship with God.[17] Unfortunately, this meant that we could rebel, eat the forbidden fruit, and turn away from God. Were we *creatio automata*, Adam and Eve would still be in the garden, never having sinned, and theologies and ecclesiologies would not be necessary.

For God, it was a risk to create humans ultimately free because this freedom opened up a possibility for rebellion and defections. God did not plan for evil to happen, but evil was the risk of free agency. Even though God took the risk of making evil possible, it was not God's will for evil to happen. Pinnock argues that "things do not always go the way God wants them to. For the sake of love, God created a world that would require tremendous resourcefulness on God's part and radical trust on ours."[18] This freedom requires God to work with "tremendous resourcefulness," as Pinnock puts it, to always inspire, call, and lure creation to love and do good instead of turning away and creating evils. When evil happens, God still tries to squeeze some good from evil. For us, this freedom requires a "radical trust" that God is still with us and calls us to love even though evils are a part of our experience.

Trust is rudimentary in relationships. To be in a true relationship with God, we need to trust God, and maybe more radically, God needs to trust us. A healthy relationship cannot exist without trust! One of the radical views of ORT is that God trusts creation to love, enact good virtues, and live a good life. In giving humans

---

17. Gen. 2:4-3:24

18. Pinnock, *MOST MOVED MOVER*, 132.

freedom, God is divinely self-limited, so God needs to build relationships with humans to inspire and lure them to act out God's
will on earth. Professor of Theology and relational theologian
Curtis Holtzen explores trust in his book with the very saying
name *The God who Trusts*. Here, he quotes the Canadian philosopher Trudy Govier[19] when he elaborates, "Relationships are built
upon trust, for when we trust, 'we are more likely to let ourselves
be vulnerable to others, to allow ourselves, to depend on others, to
cooperate, to confide.' Thus, there is no intimacy without trust."[20]

God trusts us to be in relation with God but cannot control
us. Therefore, God risks rejection. God needs our relationship
and trust to act out God's plans and power here on earth because
God is divinely self-limited. What divine self-limitation looks like
and what it means for ORT will be the subject of the next chapter.

---

19. Trudy Govier, *Dilemmas of Trust* (Montreal ; Ithaca: McGill-Queen's University
Press, 1998), 6.

20. Holtzen, *The God Who Trusts*, 132.

Amipotence

An important point in ORT is the redefinition of omnipotence. According to ORT, God is omnipotent *but* limited, so there are things God cannot logically do. For example, God cannot create a rock so heavy that God cannot lift it. That would not be sensible. In the same way, God cannot act contrary to the essence/experience binate, nor can God overrule creaturely freedom for a thing cannot be called free if it can be overruled. Oord states that "[b]ased on the enormous number of necessary qualifications [needed for omnipotence] the phrase should be dead [...] omnipotence dies a death by a thousand qualifications."[1] To clarify ORT's view on omnipotence, Oord has coined the word *amipotence*. This means that God's power is limited by God's essence, which is love.[2]

It is important to add that the spectrum of thinkers within ORT varies significantly on this question. Pinnock would, for example, argue that God cannot act single-handedly and coerce, except in some instances when God suddenly decides to do so anyway, which we call miracles. On the other hand, Oord will only accept a logically coherent theology. Therefore, Oord will

1. Thomas Jay Oord, *The Death of Omnipotence and Birth of Amipotence* (U.S.A.: Sacrasage Press, 2023), 74.

2. Oord, *Open and Relational Theology*.

explain miraculous healing by saying that the cells in the body cooperated with God and healed, extending free agency to the smallest entities of the universe. For this book, I mainly work with Oord's view of ORT and argue that God cannot, in any circumstance, act single-handedly.

To understand amipotence, we need to start with the God who trusts us. ORT argues that God divinely self-limits to give creation freedom and agency. In giving us the power of freedom, God essentially self-limits and gives up power. God doesn't control or ensure certain decisions are made; instead, God presents us with ultimate freedom. God cannot overrule this freedom, as that would not be in accordance with God's loving essence. Holtzen says, "To give power is to give up power. Even God cannot give us power, that is, freedom to make our own decisions, and yet guarantee that every decision we make will be exactly as God desires."[3] The amipotent God has the power to do everything within God's essence. But it limits God's ability to control creatures. Giving up power makes loving relationships with creation possible. God cannot turn back on this giving of power.

Process theologian Bernard Loomer also makes the case that an unlimited omnipotent God has become an idol of our culture. We idolize a god who can perfect our lives with a finger snap. A god that you cannot doubt because the god is so perfect that there is no room for doubt. Loomer calls this the god of unilateral power and says, "It is a universal god. But it is a demonic god, an idol which is not large enough to merit our faith and devotion. The issue appears to be in doubt. But the faith which can live with that doubt is a steadfast and hopeful trust in both the goodness and the power of a relational god of adequate size."[4] Loomer argues that a relational and amipotent view of God makes it possible

---

3. Holtzen, *The God Who Trusts*, 63.
4. Bernard Loomer, 'Two Conceptions of Power', *Process Studies* 6, no. 1 (1976): 5–32.

for a faith that is steadfast and holds a place for doubt. We can have faith that the relational God wants to see goodness and love flow even though evils arise in the world.

As mentioned earlier, Oord coined the term *amipotence* to frame this relational powered God: a God that self-limits to ensure our freedom and acts through love. Oord defines amipotence like this: "An amipotent God is active, but not a dictator. Amipotence is receptive but not overwhelmed. It engages without domineering, is generous but not pushy, and invites without monopolizing. Amipotence is divine strength working positively at all times and places. The power of an amipotent God is the power of love."[5] Therefore, amipotence redefines God's power as a power that solely works through love! This means that the power of God is limited to actions that are in accordance with love to promote overall well-being. It also signifies that the amipotent God cannot act single-handedly in the physically localized world. Love is not a physical and localized power. Love cannot stop a bullet or heal cancer. But love can inspire and lure leaders to forgive and stop the war and motivate doctors to give their patients the correct treatment.

Jürgen Moltmann makes a similar claim. Though he did not know of the word *amipotence* at the time he wrote the following, he draws a very similar conclusion and says, "Creation proceeds from God's love, and this love respects the particular existence of all things, and the freedom of the human beings who have been created. [...] It is not God's power that is almighty. What is almighty is his love."[6] Moltmann separates God's power from God's love and states that omnipotence is not about the power of God but God's love. While this sounds good, it does place God

---

5. Oord, *Open and Relational Theology*, 81.

6. Jürgen Moltmann, 'God's Kenosis in the Creation and Consummation of the World', in *The Work of Love: Creation as Kenosis*, ed. John Polkinghorne (Eerdmans, 2001), 147–49.

in a power/love duality, meaning that love is trying to manage the power of God so God will not cause evil. A critique of amipotence is that it leads to an impotent God. If God cannot act single-handedly and overrule creaturely action, then how can God act at all? Why pray for miracles when God is made impotent by self-limitation?

ORT argues that God's love is uncontrolling and is, therefore, self-giving and others-empowering. This does not make God impotent, hence the definition of amipotence. God does not control but acts out of love to inspire, call, and lure creation to follow God's path and plan. From the perspective of ORT, when we pray for a miracle, we should pray that God will inspire doctors and scientists to find the best treatment for our sick neighbor. It is not that God will single-handedly remove cancer, but God will call doctors to their profession, inspire them to practice and develop better treatments, etc. God works in all ways amipotence permits to prevent evil, but we cannot pray for God to single-handedly prevent all evils and expect results while we lean back. Oord says that "a relational God of uncontrolling love can't singlehandedly prevent evil done by free creatures, smaller organisms, or inanimate sources. A loving God without the ability to control can't be rightly blamed for causing or allowing evil. God can't prevent evil singlehandedly."[7] ORT argues that God's amipotence means God's love is uncontrolling. God, therefore, needs partners to function as God's body in this physical world to prevent evil.

Oord also states that "[a]mipotence affirms the existence of a powerful God whose universal influence is uncontrolling love."[8] The amipotent God works in every possible way with the

---

7. Oord, *Open and Relational Theology*, 85.

8. Oord, *The Death of Omnipotence and Birth of Amipotence*, 150.

framework of the uncontrolling love of God to create good and overall well-being. This is done in relationship to the rest of creation and with the free agency of creation to be God's hands and feet.

We shall now move on and look at the topic of prayer and how humans can cooperate with the amipotent God.

Cooperation and prayer

As mentioned earlier, a major critique of ORT is that God becomes impotent, aloof, and not able to act in the world. ORT responds to this critique in terms of amipotence and that God is calling creation to cooperate. This then raises a new set of questions: How do we cooperate with the Divine? And why pray when God cannot act single-handedly in the world? In this chapter, we will start by looking at why and how we should pray in the view of ORT and move on to look at cooperation with the Divine.

ORT argues that God should not be encountered as a divine ruler with whom we can plead our case. God should be encountered as a friend, in whom we can trust and confide. The Swiss theologian Karl Barth puts it like this: "The Grace of God to sinful man is that [God] encounters him as the hearing God; that [God] calls him not merely to the humility of a servant and the thankfulness of a child but to the intimacy and boldness of a friend."[1] Though Barth himself is not within ORT, this quote is often referred to, as it hits the nail on the head for thinkers within ORT. They argue that God's grace to us is that God is always

1. Karl Barth, *The Doctrine of Creation. p. 3: Vol. 3. The Doctrine of Creation*, vol. 3 (London: Clark, 2004), 285.

present to listen and that we are not primarily servants but instead called to be real friends of God.

This is also shown in the gospels. Both Luke and John make the case that our friendship with God is the basis on which we can pray to God. Moltmann picks up on this and says it poetically: "A man may feel himself to be God's servant in obedience to the commandments. He may see himself as the child of God through faith in the Gospel. But in prayer, he talks to God as to his friend."[2] In prayer, we encounter God as a friend. Here's one example from Luke: After teaching us the Lord's Prayer, Jesus goes on to tell a parable about a request for a piece of bread. Although very inconvenient for the other party, he still fulfills the request and gives the man some bread for the sake of the friendship.[3] Jesus shows us how they encounter God through friendship, understanding, and love. And in John, Jesus tells us that we are no more servants of God. Jesus calls us to a close relationship, saying, "Instead, I have called you friends."[4]

To try and link these ideas of how we pray to how we cooperate with God, consider the following example. Imagine someone who needs a grand piano moved, asking a friend, "Will you move a grand piano for me?" The friend might respond by saying, "I would like to help, but I can't move that thing alone." Despite his friend's response, the piano owner asks again. And twice on the following day. And then he pulls his church community in on the request. Imagine all of them calling the poor friend, pleading and believing that asking with more intensity and frequency will somehow make the friend able to move that grand piano single-handedly. It simply would not make any sense.

---

2. Moltmann, *The Church in the Power of the Spirit*, 118.

3. Luke 11:5-9

4. John 15:15

But what if the person called up his friend and said, "Will you come over tomorrow and help me move the grand piano? Maybe you even have some tools or a hand trolley to help us along the way?" In the same way, we cannot pray to God for a single-handed solution. We need to cooperate with the Divine, to ask for inspiration and for God to inspire others so that we can overcome our challenges together. ORT argues that we should pray for inspiration on how to cooperate with the Divine.

There is a need to cooperate because the main restraint of God is that God does not have a localized body to act in the world. There is not a localized physical God-body somewhere over the clouds. Humans can use their hands to help move a grand piano. They can use their hands to pull back a child before it walks out on the road just in front of a speeding lorry and save the child from harm. But God does not have such a localized body. Oord says "God inspires humans to use their own bodies to show love. When they cooperate with divine inspiration, they become God's metaphorical hands and feet. But unlike humans, the omnipresent Spirit doesn't have a localized body."[5] God can act in this world through my hands and feet. By inspiring me and the rest of creation to use their localized entities, God can amipotently be present with creation, work for good, and promote overall well-being.

The idea of divine cooperation is interwoven through all the iterations of process theology, open theism, and ORT. For Whitehead, who was the primary man behind process theology, the main idea was that love has causal efficacy in creation. Mesle, who has done a great amount of work laying out Whitehead's ideas in a more understandable language, explains it like this:

The flow of experience constituting your conscious and un-conscious self—including your love for others—also participates

---

5. Oord, *Open and Relational Theology*, 83–84.

in the causal web of life as both effect and cause. That means that your experience of love can move your hands and arms to touch with gentleness, to hug with protectiveness, to reach out to others in ways that enact the causal power of your love in the world.[6]

To try and make Whitehead's ideas a bit more understandable, I might say it this way: ultimate love is given to us through God so that we are fully shaped through love. As Oord points out, love is not only a warm fuzzy feeling on the inside but an active power of good in the world that promotes overall well-being. This love can move my hands and feet to reach out and enact the causal power of love, as Mesle puts it. Love is God's primary way of inspiring and moving humans. Love creates empathy, understanding, a will to change unfair structures, and the ability to stand up for the defenseless. Love makes us "act intentionally, in relational response to God and others, to promote overall well-being,"[7] as Oord defines it.

This is what Whitehead calls *the Eros of the universe*. The divine Eros is the lure and calling that all creatures feel to spread God's love. Keller notes that "[Whitehead] had in mind a cosmic appetite for becoming, for beauty and intensity of experience. The divine Eros is felt in each creature as the 'initial aim'—or the 'lure.' It is a lure to our own becoming, a call to actualize the possibilities for greater beauty and intensity in our own lives."[8] This divine Eros calls us, attracts us, and invites us into becoming and actualizing our possibilities to create greater beauty and overall well-being. The postmodern theologian John D. Caputo would define this as the "Folly of God," saying, "The Folly of God is that God does not exist [physically]. God insists, but God does

---

6. C. Robert Mesle, *Process-Relational Philosophy: An Introduction to Alfred North Whitehead* (West Conshohocken, Pa: Templeton Foundation Press, 2008), 64.

7. Oord, *Pluriform Love: An Open and Relational Theology of Well-Being*, 28.

8. Keller, *On the Mystery*, 99.

not exist."[9] Though Caputo is more within radical and "weak" theology than ORT, he surely does share the view of God being more amipotent than omnipotent. God works with and through creatures by insisting on or luring us to cooperate.

So, ORT argues that God needs our cooperation because God does not have a physical existence or a localized body of any form. God, therefore, needs our bodies, our physical existence, for physical, localized actions. Therefore, ORT argues that God cannot stop evil single-handedly, but God can stop evil when we or other creaturely entities cooperate. Oord argues that "God calls creatures and creation to join the work to overcome evil. Although unable to stop evil single-handedly, God can stop it when we or others cooperate with the divine work of love. The Creator needs creation's partnership."[10] Within ORT, there are different views on whether free agency and cooperation are reserved for larger, more complicated entities (animals, humans, etc.) or whether the smallest cells, atoms, and subatomic particles can also choose to cooperate or not. For this book, I will not go further into that discussion, as my focus is on ecclesiology and human beings. It is important to note here that our lives gain real significance because they are essential to God's endeavors in creating a good world. We need to cooperate to act out God's plan to which God invites us.

In other words, the Creator and creation are forever interdependent. We creatures are utmost dependent on God for our mere existence, and simultaneously, God has given us the freedom to be in real relationships. There, God needs our freely chosen relationship and cooperation to act out God's plans for this world. We can choose not to cooperate, and hence, God's plans will ultimately fail. Holtzen writes, "God has become dependent

---

9. John D. Caputo, *The Folly of God: A Theology of the Unconditional* (Salem, Oregon: Polebridge Press, 2016), 78.

10. Oord, *Open and Relational Theology*, 86.

upon humans in the furtherance of the purposes in the world. All creations have a God-given vocation within God's creation-wide telos. Therefore, God has freely chosen to rely on that which is not divine to engage and accomplish divine purposes."[11] God depends on creatures to further take part in co-creating creation, so to speak. But God takes the risk that God's plan does not pan out. It is inherent in creating us as free agents. ORT, therefore, argues that we must seek God through prayer for inspiration and challenges to live out God's plans here on earth, to be the living body of God through cooperation with the Divine.

---

11. Holtzen, *The God Who Trusts*, 142–43.

Flow of time

Another important point for ORT concerns God's experience and the flow of time. Often, theologians will argue that God exists outside of time and does not experience time the same way we do. This is usually explained with the image that God can view the entire timeline at once in the same way we observe a one-dimensional line. But ORT differs here, arguing that if God can view the entire timeline from start to end, then the future is settled; therefore, creatures are not free agents. ORT argues that this does not fit into a scriptural understanding of God, as explained in earlier chapters. ORT will instead argue that God experiences the flow of time in the exact same way that we creatures do. What is past for us is past for God. What is present to us is present to God, and neither creatures nor Creator can foresee the future.

Back in the introduction, I included an image in which Oord compares God to a jazz bandleader. This image shows us how ORT sees the flow of time. To ORT, life is like a jazz session. Contrary to the classical concerto—where every single note is pre-recorded and the musician only plays what is planned for them, led by the conductor—the jazz session is not preplanned. This does not mean that life is completely chaotic. Like the jazz session, life has a certain framework and trajectory. There is a common beginning, and all of us look toward some sort of ending, though it is not yet completely defined. We play in a certain key around a certain theme. But we can all freestyle, play a solo, alter the mood of the music, or choose our path within the framework. The inspiring Bandleader listens and then guides, nudges, and coaxes us to a certain expression. The Bandleader does not tell us exactly what to play but creates a space for us to be creative and free. Oord puts it like this:

Nothing and no one—not even God—prerecords history. The future is open and yet to be determined. We're all in process. Life isn't absolutely chaotic. It has patterns and regularities, habits and structures. Love, truth, and beauty are real goals with real influence. Existence isn't 'anything goes.' [...] The [jazz band] Leader experiences the music as it happens, along with everyone else, uncertain where the tune will go. It's experimental, not prearranged.[1]

ORT argues that God must experience time the same way creation does for creation to be truly free. If not, God could foreknow all our actions, and we would not be truly free. This also demands a redefinition of God's omniscience; ORT would argue that God can know everything that is presently knowable. God cannot know the future, as it is not presently knowable and therefore not in God's omniscience. Whether I turn left or right is completely up to me as a free agent and is only known by God as I make the turn.

Based on this metaphor, it makes sense to think of the future as an ever-evolving process. Some parts may be partly settled or planned, just like the jazz session, where we have a trajectory that loosely points toward a common end. It is not set in stone. It is partly settled and partly unsettled. Some things are still to come. There is a framework, a rhythm, and a groove, but the tune is still maturing and developing. Pinnock calls the future *a realm of possibilities, not just of actualities*, and notes, that "[t]his is true

---

1. Oord, *Open and Relational Theology*, 27–28.

even for God, though his awareness of the future possibilities and his anticipation of the future actualities is hugely greater than our own. Nevertheless, the future is open for God as well because everything is not yet settled."[2] God has a greatly larger perspective of where we all are going, just like the inspiring jazz bandleader has a great overview of the individual members of the band and can nudge us toward a common end. God oversees all parts of creation and knows everything presently knowable. This makes God able to make a trajectory and invite and lure us along the way.

Mesle, building on Whitehead, also points out that if all of time is pre-settled by God, then we are nothing but a mere dot in the enormous tapestry of God's preplanned timeline. This is a very static view of time, in which there is only one possible way forward, pre-settled by the Divine ruler. Drawing inspiration from process philosophy, ORT argues that the future timeline is not static, but dynamic and moldable. We can change tomorrow with the action we take today. Mesle writes, "if God created the tapestry of time, with the whole world story on it, we had and have nothing to say about what God decided we would do. Whatever is going to happen has already happened. [...] Being is real, but becoming is a kind of illusion experienced only by us finite creatures within time."[3] If the timeline was static, then we could be *beings*, but all of our life is already settled. Therefore, we could not *become*. Becoming would be an illusion only experienced by us finite creatures. We cannot *become* because we already *are*!

In the static view of time, the future has happened. God has settled it. Everything that happens, all of our so-called choices, are mere illusions on the settled tapestry of time. So, for creation to be completely free agents, the future timeline must be dynamic, leaving the future open. Therefore, God cannot foreknow the

---

2. Pinnock, *MOST MOVED MOVER*, 51.

3. Mesle, *Process-Relational Philosophy*, 6.

future and must experience the flow of time just like the rest of creation. Oord also argues that "God experiences the flow of time too. The past is the past for God, and not even God can change it. The present is present, and the future is open. A Living Lover who creates, empowers, inspires, and helps also experiences reality moment by moment. Creator and creation are in process."[4] The "Open" in ORT implies that all of creation is in a never-ending process with the Creator, where we work together to co-create the future.

This also implies that history is a combined product created by the Creator and creation together. As God does not only influence creatures but creatures also influence God through prayer etc., a true co-creation process can take place. Pinnock argues that "God's will is not the ultimate explanation for everything that happens; human decisions and actions make an important contribution too. Thus history is the combined result of what God and [God's] creatures decide to do."[5] When creation and Creator work together, we are actually able to change the chain of events. History is not a mere record of God's work in the world, but the greatest record of divine and creaturely co-creation.

Mesle agrees that creatures create the present moment by moment. Furthermore, he notes that the future does not yet exist. Instead, the future must be created by creatures taking action and bringing each new moment into being. Mesle writes, "Decisions must be made; the future must be created. The creatures of the present must decide between many possibilities for what may happen, and their collective decisions bring the new moment into being."[6] At any given moment, we have a set of possible actions in front of us. God will inspire and lure us to choose the

---

4. Oord, *Open and Relational Theology*, 29.

5. Pinnock, *The Openness of God*, 15–16.

6. Mesle, *Process-Relational Philosophy*, 7.

actions that create overall well-being. We can choose otherwise. And sometimes, we can choose what seems right, but it turns out wrong. At present, creatures must decide how to move forward. ORT argues that God does not know what happens in the next moment; it depends on creaturely decisions and actions.

Many theologians would disagree with these views, saying that ORT diminishes or makes God impotent because God cannot control the future. This critique will often raise questions of why and how we can get prophetic words if the future is open. How could Jesus come to be if God did not plan for him to fulfill the role of messiah, etc.? ORT defends this by pointing out that many prophecies are contingent, and not all prophecies see fulfillment. God could have a plan for a future chain of events. If all creatures cooperate in this plan, the prophecy will be fulfilled. Therefore, Christ was a plan which worked due to creaturely and divine cooperation.

According to ORT, God is not able to foreknow that any of the plans will pan out. If God did, then the future would be closed, and creatures would not live in a realm of life options and creative choices. Instead, our lives would be preprogrammed to follow God's plan. If we take it to be true that creation ultimately has free agency, then creatures must be able to diverge from God's plan. If the future is divinely foreknown, then creatures cannot diverge.

Oord says, "Instead of being able to make free decisions about life and love, we're merely experiencing a simulation like the Matrix. A settled future is inconsistent with our freely choosing. If God foreknows all, freedom, love, and randomness are myths."[7] This also implies that God's knowledge is confined within the flow of time. God is omniscient in the sense that God knows all that is possibly knowable. But it would be illogical to assume God

---

7. Oord, *Open and Relational Theology*, 33–34.

could know what is unknowable. Oord says that "[n]o one—not even God—can know what's unknowable. If something isn't knowable, it can't be known. There is no there there."[8]

In this statement, Oord agrees with Pinnock, who notes that God cannot know what has not yet come into being, saying that "God does not foreknow every future choice or the outcome of every human decision. God is all-knowing in the sense that he knows all that it is possible to know and powerful enough to do whatever is needed."[9] ORT argues that the flow of time limits God's omnipotence to only knowing what is presently knowable. This again builds on creaturely free agency. Could God foreknow your actions tomorrow, then they would have, in some sense, already happened. The actions would be predetermined, and you would not be free.

For ORT, God is logically omniscient, meaning God can know all that is presently knowable. Much in the same way, ORT argues that God is logically omnipotent as long as it concerns coherent actions within God's essence. This all comes down to how the flow of time is viewed. To ORT, God and humans experience the flow of time moment by moment at the same rate. What is past for creation is also the past for God, etc. This is important because if God could see into the future, then creaturely actions would be pre-settled or planned to some effect. For creation to be truly free so that it can be in a true relationship with the Divine, God must be limited within the same scope of time as creation, although God is able to know everything that is presently knowable and is, in that way, logically omniscient.

---

8. Oord, 36.

9. Pinnock, *The Openness of God*, 124.

In the simplest sense...

To conclude this section, I will summarize this introduction to ORT. The development of ORT has been fueled by a longing for a theological framework that takes scripture seriously and makes logical sense in our lives and the faith we express as communities.

Essentially, scripture places a lot of weight on God being love and God wanting real relationships with creation. For this, God must give up power and, retract God's being and make room for free creaturely agency. ORT argues for God's amipotence—that God's power is love and that God calls, lures, and invites all of creation to partake in the work of love. Creatures have free agency, implying that the future is not yet settled. God has no plans for every single point in time. Instead, God experiences the flow of time together with creation. ORT argues that God makes plans for the best possible future and calls creation to cooperate with this plan. God's plans must often fail due to creaturely non-cooperation. Therefore, God must change paths and come up with new plans. We can partake in God's plans and co-create by offering our agency for God's plans. When we pray, we supply God with information on where we are and what we can contribute and ask for divine inspiration on where our part in God's ongoing creation is. ORT argues that praying makes us better co-creators.

In the simplest sense, God is open and relational because God wants real relationships with creation. Therefore, creatures must have free agency, and God cannot foreknow the future but works to inspire, call, and lure all of creation to co-create God's plans for love and overall well-being.

PART THREE

Open and Relational Ecclesiology

Building the Basileia –
An Open and Relational Ecclesiology

So far, I have looked at what defines ecclesiology, and I have given an introduction to the field of ORT. Now, the question stands: How do we construct an ecclesiology from ORT, and what separates this ecclesiology from others? For this part, I will explore what I see should define ORE and in what ways we can work practically with ORE. Overall, it is important that ORE, as well as ORT, will be robust theology that makes sense of both our theology and lived experience and that is coherent. ORE should rightly frame how we can live a communal life as co-creators of the Creator's masterpiece and be practical enough for us to put it into action.

Moving forward, this is also the part of the book where I will construct new understanding and knowledge based on my introductions to ecclesiology and ORT. In the following construction of ORE, I will point back to the areas that I have discussed earlier, linking the introduction to ecclesiology to the ideas of ORT. I will continue to put some extra perspectives on ORE and deepen some of my points by drawing in a couple of thoughts from theologians and thinkers within ORT who have touched on the subject of ORE. As stated earlier, there has been no deeper work done in the area of ORE. Some theologians may have touched on the subject, but there have not, to the best of my knowledge, been any complete works on ORE. In this part of the book, we shall start to turn toward constructing ORE and see what it might look like. This is where we will explore what steps we can take to move toward ORE.

This construction of ORE will start with a brief overview of what must be the focus of ORE and why I choose to call this part *Building the Basileia*, focusing on that one word: *Basileia*, which is Greek for "the Kingdom of God." After that, I have two theological legs that must be respected in ORE: firstly, the Church is *in, but not of* the world, and secondly, the call to be *co-creators*. From those two theological legs, I will draw forth three major practical outputs of ORE that are essential in building a community based on ORT.

The first aspect concerns the mission of the Church, which, in ORE, is to take seriously our responsibility as co-creators and caretakers of creation. As free agents, they will be inspired and lured by God into loving and creating overall well-being.

The second and third aspects are more concerned with the nature of the Church. The second aspect is that the Church in ORE must acknowledge relationships as a divine structure. ORE should both be working to enrich interpersonal relationships and create a space for deepening divine relationships. This calls for relational leadership to be embraced in Churches.

And the third aspect is that by building on love and true relationships, ORE should work to be inclusive for all people from all different walks of life. This radical inclusiveness is important because God is present in all creation and all beings.

All of these chapters will be focused on how to embrace ORE in a congregation, meaning that I will make these chapters as practical as possible so that the knowledge I provide can easily be put to good use.

15.1 What is the goal?

Before we dig deeper into ORE, we need to look at the overall goal or mission of the Church. What is the point of the congregation? Why do we gather as Christians in Churches?

The overall goal for ORE is to be co-creators together with the Creator. ORT teaches us that God is in an everlasting creative process to deepen and evolve the universe. God constantly calls and lures us to be part of the creation process. God wants us to co-create creation in a relational response to God and others. (See Chapter 12, Cooperation and Prayer.) Ever since Eden, this has been our task as human beings. And more than just caring for or tending to creation, we are also building the Kingdom of God. We are also pulling the being of God into the present every day through loving our neighbor, discipling Christ, and working to share the Good News with everyone. The so-called "good virtues" of Christianity, (i.e., empathy, loving our neighbor, being humble and kind of heart, etc.) are the quintessential tools for practically building the Basileia in our world today.

In other words, the task of ORE is to build the Kingdom of God now while pointing toward the Kingdom yet to come. The mission is to install a rule in our world right now, in which the culture builds on the divine love of God by cooperating with the Divine and following God's plans and lures for us. The community of the Church should be the power center, in which we together seek God for inspiration on where to go and how to cooperate, as well as being a community that actively builds the rule, or Kingdom, of God already today.

Looking back at Dulles's models of the Church, this has a clear flavor of the Church as Servant. The community of the Church is seen as the active force that creates a better reality, in the present, today. As we get further through this part of the book, I will deepen this connection between ORE and the Church as servant.

Therefore, I choose to frame ORE under the phrase *Building the Basileia,* as this is the mission statement for ORE: to be co-creators of the Kingdom of God and to be working for the rule of God. Before we go too deep into this, I want to use some paragraphs explaining what I understand by the term "the Kingdom of God."

15.2 | Defining *Basileia*

The Greek phrase used in the bible is *βασιλεία τοῦ Θεοῦ* (Basileia Tou Theou), meaning "The Kingdom of God." βασιλεία appears 162 times in the NT and most times denotes the Kingdom of God (τοῦ Θεοῦ) or the Kingdom of Heaven (τῶν Οὐρανῶν)[1]. The Kingdom of God or Heaven is used quite interchangeably, especially by the writer of the gospel of Matthew, who uses the "Kingdom of Heaven" often but switches to the "Kingdom of God" without any consistency.[2]

I will use "the Kingdom of God" as it is more precise and specifies that God is in the center of this kingdom. When we speak of the Kingdom of Heaven, it often denotes an outdated imagery of a three-tiered universe with a heavenly realm on top and an under earthly realm below. The Basileia is not to be understood as a distant world but an actual ruling of God right now. Here, we also need to tread carefully. There is an inherent danger in thinking of a Kingdom or a Ruling of God as a landmass or physical place. Indeed, kingdom in the English language often denotes something like a country or a land area. Basileia, on the other hand, does not mainly refer to a country but is more often

---

1. Bible Hub, 'Strong's Greek: 932. Βασιλεία (Basileia)—Kingdom, Sovereignty, Royal Power', 2022, https://biblehub.com/greek/932.htm.

2. Mogens Müller, *Kommentar til Matthæusevangeliet*, Dansk kommentar til Det nye Testamente 3 (Århus: Aarhus Universitetsforl, 2000).

used to describe the might of a King or to indicate what a King rules over in terms of people, wealth, etc.[3]

In the NT, Jesus uses "Kingdom of God" or "Kingdom of Heaven" many times. The phrase is sometimes used in the epistles as well, though with slight variations (i.e., the Kingdom of the Father, Lord, etc.)[4] The following quotes are examples from the Gospel of Matthew, where Jesus describes the Basileia. Jesus often uses the word in parables or metaphors. For example, "The kingdom of heaven is like a mustard seed..."[5] or "The kingdom of heaven is like a king who prepared a wedding banquet for his son."[6] And finally, Jesus uses it as a simple statement: "Let the little children come to me, and do not hinder them, for the kingdom of heaven belongs to such as these."[7]

It is important to note that most often, Jesus uses Basileia in an active sense, not as a static country but as an active rule of God, caring for all of creation. In the parables of the weeds, mustard seeds, and yeast,[8] it is clear that Jesus denotes a ruling of the King, of God, and not a country. Jesus says that the Basileia is like the farmer sowing the seeds and then weeding them out. Or like the little mustard seed or grain of yeast, which seems small but has

---

3. C. Berg, *Oldgræsk-dansk Ordbog*, 3. udgave (Kbh.: Gyldendal, 2003), 125.

4. Apperances in the NT for those of you who like to nerd out: βασιλεία τῶν οὐρανῶν (Kingdom of Heaven): Matt. 3:2, 4:17, 5:3.10.19.20, 7:21, 8:11, 10:7, 11:11.12, 13:11.24.31.33.44.45.47.52, 16:19 18:1.3.4.23, 19:12.14.23.24, 20:1, 21:43, 22:2, 23:13, 25:1. βασιλεία τοῦ Θεοῦ (Kingdom of God): Matt. 6:33, 21:31, Mark 1:15, 4:11.26.30, 9:1.47, 10:14.15.23.24.25, 12:34, 14:25, 15:43, Luke 4:43, 6:20, 7:28, 8:1.10, 9:2.11.27.60.62, 10:9.11, 11:20, 13:18.20.28.29, 14:15, 16:16, 17:20.21, 18:16.17.24.25.29, 19:11, 21:31, 22:16.18, 23:51, John 3:5, Acts 1:3, 8:12, 14:22, 19:8, 28:23.31, Romans 14:17, 1. Cor. 4:20, 6:9.10, 15:24.50, Gal. 5:31, Col. 4:11, 2 Thess. 1:5, Eph. 5:5, Rev. 12:10. βασιλεία τοῦ πατρὸς (Fathers Kingdom): Mark 11:10. βασιλείαν αὐτοῦ (His Kingdom): 2. Tim. 4:1.18. βασιλείαν τοῦ κυρίου (Kingdom of the Lord): 2. Pet. 1:11. βασιλείαν τοῦ Υἱοῦ (Kingdom of the Son): Col. 1:13

5. Matt. 13:31

6. Matt. 22:2

7. Matt. 19:14

8. Matt. 13:24-34

enormous power. The Basileia is a dynamic action more than a static mass. And in the next verses, Jesus then reverses the parables and says that the Basileia is like a hidden treasure, a pearl, and a fishing net.[9] Again, these aim at the Basileia being God's rule in this world, reaching out to creation, wanting a relationship, and calling for creation to cooperate.[10]

Furthermore, Basileia infers that something has already started happening and will continue into the future. The Kingdom, or Ruling of God, is already actively working in this world, has always been working, and will always be working. Suppose one looks over all 162 appearances of Basileia in the NT, like the examples I gave from the Gospel of Matthew. In that case, it is clear that Basileia signifies something already happening: a mustard seed planted in the world or a person in the present. At the same time, this seed will sprout from there into the future. Therefore, there is a sense of something that is still to come. Jesus also uses these "future" metaphors for the Basileia. It is easier to get the camel through the eye of the needle than for a rich person to get into the Kingdom into the presence and under the rule of God.[11]

For ORE, these are important aspects! We are presently building something in our communities—some flicker of the great Kingdom of God, a flicker of God's very being that shines through our communities. And yet, something is not yet present to us. We still point beyond ourselves toward the coming Kingdom. The Church not only inaugurates the Kingdom today but is also a sign toward the future Kingdom, the realm of God that is to come, the realm that God must eschatologically fulfill

---

9. Matt. 13:44-50

10. Geert Hallbäck and Hans Jørgen Lundager Jensen, *Gads bibel leksikon*, 2. udgave [1-bindsudgave] (Kbh.: Gad, 2011), 267–68; Müller, *Kommentar til Matthæusevangeliet*, 315–30.

11. Luke 18:25

at some point.[12] The eschatological hope of the future Kingdom cannot be a static "plan." As God is open and creatures are free, God must constantly work to readjust the eschatological plan for fulfilling the future Kingdom.

For this book, I need to specify that I will speak of Basileia as the Kingdom of God, meaning the rule of God here on earth already now. This is the language that Jesus uses in scripture, which we will continue in ORE. The Basileia is an active interaction and not a passive landmass in some unknown location. This ruling of God as the King draws many parallels to the monarchies in Scandinavia. Our Danish queen does not single-handedly rule the country. Her role here is to serve the people. Actually, she has no real ability to single-handedly carry out any order or infer any laws on her own. Our queen can nudge and guide the people through speeches and acting as a moral leader. Her role as queen and her rule comes from a humble place of humility. Her role is to serve, not to be served. In the same way, the ruling of the Basileia is a humble ruling. God cannot single-handedly change a person's mind, but God has an enormous capacity to nudge and guide that person so they can cooperate and carry out the humble ruling of God.

So, in my choice of the heading *Building the Basileia* to frame ORE, the meaning is that creation can work to reinstate the love of God as the guiding rule in the universe. It does not mean that we will build an actual kingdom. It does not mean that we should create our own state with a flag, government, and politics. The actual Kingdom is not a political term but an act of bringing God's essential being into present reality. The "already" aspect of the Basileia is about building a community that uses love, which is the essence of God, as the guiding principle and that wants to spread that love to the rest of creation. In this work, there arises a

---

12. Hallbäck and Lundager Jensen, *Gads bibel leksikon*, 267–68.

"not yet" aspect, where the Church points toward the eschatolog-ical hope that all of creation will be part of the Kingdom and be closely connected to God.

This was a short introduction to why I chose the heading *Building the Basileia* as a working title for ORE. From here, we need to explore the practical theological side of building the Basileia community. I will examine the two theological observa-tions with importance for ORE, namely that the Church is in, but not of the world, and that the Church is called to co-create creation. These will lead us to the three practical outputs of ORE.

Two theological observations of the Basileia

I need to start with two very important theological observations about the Basileia before we dig into the practical side of ORE. For ORE to stand firmly in ORT, it is important to discern two key theological observations that will separate ORE from other ecclesiologies and solidly place its foundations on ORT.

Firstly, the Church is called to be in, but not of the world. This is important because the Church must always point toward a dimension of the Divine, not the earthly. The Church is sent to reconnect creation to its Creator. That is why we are building the already present Basileia and still point toward an eschatological future. Being in, but not of the world holds true the open aspect of God. It means that we have a real influence on creation.

Secondly, we must realize that the Church is creating a new creation within creation. The Church is not called to huddle up and wait for the coming of the new creation. The Church is called to start the new creation right here and now, in cooperation with God and others. The Church is an active community working to share the Good News, not just through the classic missions but through our entire lived lives. It is the acknowledgment that we take part in the actual life of God when we co-create.

I will now explore each of these aspects.

16.1 Being in, but not of the world

In the Gospel of John, we read Jesus saying, "If you belonged to the world, it would love you as its own. As it is, you do not belong to the world, but I have chosen you out of the world."[1] The Church, as in the community of Christ-followers, is chosen to be out of this world. This is what we often define as being *in*, but *not of* the world. In exactly that sense, all Christians are bearers of the Basileia. The Church is building the already present Basileia, as we are in the world. In this world, we are building the Kingdom of God, nurturing a culture of divine love, acceptance, and grace. Yet, God and the essential love do not fit into the general scheme of the world we are living in. Divine love is opposed to the worldly systems of consumerism, money, power, and might.

The Church is called to be in that worldly system but not live on its terms. Looking at the world, we see the world can sometimes be a cold, harsh place where people work against God's love. It is the job of the Church to help reconnect the cold, harsh places of the world to God once again, to reconnect so that the world can build on God's love instead of the consumerism of the world. ORE must open with this statement: that the Church is called to be in, but not of the world. The Church is pointing toward the Kingdom of God while already being a little preview of the great Kingdom to come.

This is important in the open aspect of ORT. In the present, we are already shaping the Basileia, and the future will depend on what we do and how we cooperate today. Therefore, ORE then maintains that the grace of the Church is to be in this world and be a positive change in this world. The Church must see it as its main task to transform this world into a reconnection to

---

1. John 15:19

the Divine—to be a little glimpse of God, a little glimpse of the Kingdom to come.

Keller makes an important point that the Church should neither transcend the world nor drown in the world, meaning that the Church must neither become an unreachable temple on top of the highest mountain only for the holiest to reach. Neither must the Church become just another cultural institution among many others. For Keller, the true grace of the Church is to be a resolute fish swimming in the world, being present and self-dependent. Keller writes, "The grace of the fish lies not in escaping the watery chaos but in moving with its currents. Such grace does not transcend the water (like the absolute), nor does it drown (like the dissolute): our little fish, swimming bravely on, is an icon of the resolute!"[2]

The little fish must become the icon of the Church in ORE, to swim bravely on without transcending or drowning in the world. The task at hand, for us and the Church as a whole, is thus not to escape this worldly chaos and enter into some unknown utopian heavenly solitude. The grace lies in moving with the currents of the world without transcending the sea or dissolving into the waters. The Church must be pointing toward the Basileia in such a way that the Basileia is already shown through the Church. We move with the creation that moves with God. The Church should not want to escape this world. The Church should want to revel in the currents of this world, to bask freely in this creation by God, constantly building the Basileia and pointing toward God, as well as working to reattune creation to the Creator, while being in, but not of the broken system of the world.

This notion of the Church pointing beyond itself as a symbol of eschatological hope complies with Moltmann's Christ-centered ecclesiology. For Moltmann, the main goal of the Church is to

---

2. Keller, *On the Mystery*, 47.

be the symbol of the eschatological hope for total reconciliation through Christ. ORE will push this further and state that
the Church is not just the symbol but also the active part. The
Church is not just pointing toward a future hope but steadily creating the future. This carries the open aspect of ORT. We cannot
point toward a future we hope for if the future is already settled.
We must instead create the future in cooperation with the divine
so that the world each day becomes a bit closer to the Basileia,
which is not yet. God is constantly working to build this coming
full reconciliation but can only do so if all creatures cooperate.

This process of creating the already present Basileia and instating a divine reality points the finger back at the Church. ORE will
argue that the Church cannot just scuddle in a beautiful building
with lots of coffee and wait for the second coming of Christ. That
is not what it means to be in, but not of the world. That is not the
call of the Church. ORE will argue that all Christians, who are all
part of the community of the Church, have an obligation to take
all the chances and possibilities before them to actualize building
the Basileia in this world. Boyd makes the point that the open
God gives all of us the power and responsibility to step into the
divine flow and be co-creators of the world: "The bottom line is
that life is all about possibilities. We are thinking, feeling, willing,
and personal beings only because we, like God, are beings who
can reflect on and choose between possibilities. We are fully alive
when we passionately seize them, adventurously explore them,
and define ourselves by actualizing them."[3] In ORE, the Church
is developed through grasping the possibilities that arise to build
the Basileia and actualize them. By grabbing these possibilities,
the Church and all Christians will define themselves as co-creators in God's divine plans for this world.

---

3. Boyd, *God of the Possible*, 94.

As I discussed in Chapter 12: Cooperation and Prayer, ORT argues that God needs our cooperation in this world. God needs us creatures to be God's hands and feet. ORT argues that God needs our actions in this physical world to live out God's plans. In being God's hands and feet, we are creatively taking part in creating creation, so to speak. Therefore, the Church becomes the co-creator of this world. As co-creators, the Church must be the servant of creation, as Dulles would define it. A task for the Church is to be co-creators who live out God's plans for this world and build the already present Basileia while pointing to the eschatological fulfillment in close cooperation with the Divine.

The co-creational aspect of ORE also has an eschatological undertone, as the Church is not only building this Basileia in this world but also in the time to come. When cooperating with the Divine, the Church also builds up to an eschatological endpoint. In the Pauline sense, building the Basileia is about co-creating already now but also pointing toward a future not yet comprehensible. Moltmann points out this double nature of the Church, saying that the Church does not live from the past alone. There is, of course, history and traditions. But all of those points toward the eschatological fulfillment due to the eschatological person of Christ. Moltmann states that the Church "exists as a factor of present liberation, between remembrance of his history and hope of his kingdom [...] If the eschatological orientation is lost, then remembrance decays into a powerless historical recollection of a founder at the beginning of things."[4] For Moltmann, the Church of Christ must be a messianic fellowship that seeks to always remember its history and draw it into attention. We can do that through the Bible and reading the tradition of the Church. And then, on the other hand, the messianic fellowship of the Church is also living in anticipation of the Kingdom, the Basileia.

---

4. Moltmann, *The Church in the Power of the Spirit*, 75.

If the Church does not point toward eschatological fulfillment, all it is reduced to is a mere remembrance of a long-gone founder. Moltmann again carries the Pauline notion of already, not yet. In ORE, the Church is already building the Basileia in the world and still pointing toward something greater and not yet experiencing the eschatological fulfillment of the Basileia.

The way that the Church is building the already present Basileia comes through discipling Christ and living out the only one command Christ gave us. The command to "Love the Lord your God with all your heart and with all your soul and with all your mind [and] Love your neighbour as yourself."[5] When we evangelize, we seek to spread the Good News of God's eternal and essential love incarnated in Jesus Christ, and we try to follow his command. Therefore, evangelizing is not just preaching a word, but it is actively building the Kingdom of God, building the Basileia right now. It is being a part of this world, truly being affected and invested in it while still pointing toward something greater, something that is to come, and something that is not yet "of" this world.

Moltmann sharply points out that "[h]ealing the sick, liberating the captives, and the hunger for righteousness belongs to the mission and go together with the preaching of the gospel to the poor."[6] Spreading the Good News in words and action is an act of being in, but not of, the world. The Church works on a divine level, co-creating the Basileia and instating a divine ruling of love. Loving our neighbors is just as essential to the mission, as well as preaching the word of the Gospel.

The Gospel is not a pure statement of some remote future to come. The Gospel starts to install the future right away; through the Gospel, there dawns a new creation when it is spoken and

---

5. Matt. 22:37-39

6. Moltmann, 76.

done in action. Moltmann also states that "[t]he Word is under-stood as creative power, like the Word of creation at the beginning. It affects what it says."[7] God becomes present in preaching the Word and spreading the Gospel. It is a creative activity, building the Basileia right here and now. If the Gospel does not lead to action, it is essentially dead.

Looking back at Dulles, the Church here becomes more than just the herald. It is not only about preaching and spreading the word. It is just as important to actually be a change for the better and create the already present Basileia. For ORE, preaching the Word is more about action and activity than words. As St. Francis of Assisi is often quoted saying[8] "Preach the Gospel at all times. Use words if necessary." For ORE, this is central. Preaching is not merely a result of words but of hands and feet working to attune creation with the Creator.

It is then paramount in ORE that the main focus and guiding principles are always loving, cooperating with the Divine, and building up the Basileia because that is what Jesus tells us to do. Nowhere in the gospels are we told to redeem or save anyone. That is not given as a mission to the Church. The only mission Christ gives to his disciples and the Church is to "go and make disciples of all nations, baptizing them in the name of the Father and of the Son and of the Holy Spirit, and teaching them to obey everything I have commanded you."[9] The Church is not to redeem anyone. The only task of the Church is to connect people to Christ so that Christ can redeem them. It is a call to make disciples, not a call to redeem anyone. It is a call to choose to live a life that points people to the redemption of Christ the Messiah.

---

7. Moltmann, 77.

8. It is quite unsure whether he ever really said this quote, but it do seem to fit into his theology.

9. Matt. 28:19-20

In this way, the Church partakes in redemption, but we do not do the redeeming. Keller importantly notes that "we participate in the new creation, in the renewal that is the Basileia: it begins. Never from nothing."[10] The Church is the beginning of the Basileia, not from nothing but from always renewing creation as it was before. The Church becomes partners in the renewal, as it were. The Church is co-creator of the world. Our actions and attitude to the world matter! The Church is here not to escape the world but to improve it, reconnect it to God, make disciples, and always be in cooperation with the Divine, never alone.

For Oord, loving like Jesus implies that we live a life of love because love is what establishes the Kingdom of God. This is just what John, according to Oord, means when he says, "Beloved, let us love one another because love is from God; everyone who loves is born of God and knows God. Whoever does not love does not know God, for God is love."[11] Love does not only stem from God, but love actually is God because God is love.[12] God's essence is this everlasting love, as discussed in Chapter 9: The Essence/Experience Binate; therefore, we show the very being of God in this world every time we "love." meaning every time we work to promote overall well-being in relational response to God and others. All these actions of love will promote overall well-being and reconnect creation to God and are, therefore, part of building the Basileia, part of bringing in God's ruling in this world.

To Moltmann, living a life of love becomes a sharp contrast to the world we are situated in. We are situated in a world of continuing deterioration and decline, says Moltmann, and in that, the Christian faith must show itself through a passionate love of life and existence. Furthermore, Moltmann says, "We can break

---

10. Keller, *On the Mystery*, 147.

11. 1. Jn 4:7-8 (NRSV).

12. Oord, *Pluriform Love: An Open and Relational Theology of Well-Being*, 153.

the spell of creeping acclimatization to the deterioration in the equality of life brought about by injustice, oppression and man-made catastrophes. The paralyzing feeling of helplessness must be overcome if mankind is to go on promising itself a future."[13]

In ORE, the Church must be a beacon of hope and life in an ever-deteriorating world. This does not mean that the Church should shy away from the world or build walls to protect itself. It is not a job of being countercultural or otherworldly, but rather, it is the task of re-culturizing the world to reconnect it to Christ, recreating the deteriorated culture to the culture of God to be rooted in the Kingdom of God and the essential love of God.

ORE acknowledges that the Church is in, but not of, the world. This is not a reason to retract and not interact with the world. Rather, it is a call to re-culturize the world into the culture of the Basileia. In the models of Dulles (Chapter 3), this ecclesiology is firmly set in the Church as Servant. The Church is here to serve the world around it and God in true and real relationships with both. The servants are focused on discipling Christ and living a life as Christ commanded us: Loving God with all of our heart, soul, and mind and our neighbors as ourselves. It is important to recognize this structure. The Church is called to serve. As Jesus tells us, "The greatest among you will be your servant. For those who exalt themselves will be humbled, and those who humble themselves will be exalted."[14] In serving not only each other but also the world, the Church shows the true loving character of God. And this is shown in a way that is completely countercultural in our consumerist culture, where the ego always takes the main stage. To serve the world lovingly is exactly what it means to be in, but not of, the world.

---

13. Moltmann, *The Church in the Power of the Spirit*, 166.

14. Matt. 23:11-12

To summarize, ORE calls the Church to be *in*, but *not of,* the world. The Church is called to be a restorative movement that constantly seeks to call out unhealthy structures of the world and reconnect these with the divine love of God. The task at hand is to create disciples that will follow Christ and, by the working of Christ, be redeemed. The eschatological hope is to see all of creation reconnected to God. That is the primary task and theological standpoint of the Church.

16.2   The call to continual co-creation

The call is to continually co-create the new creation together with the Spirit of the Creator. In other words, the mission of the Church is ultimately to be part of bringing in, or rather creating, the Basileia. As noted earlier, the word *basileia* has two basic meanings: it can be read as either the actual Kingdom of God in this world, or it can be read more as the eschatological goal of God's divine ruling to come. The challenge for the Church is to hold both these meanings at the same time. We will be struck blindsided by only reading Basileia as God's actual ruling right now or if we see it only as God's lordship in God's perfect Kingdom. Both these aspects are important to understanding the Kingdom of God and its meaning and effect on the Church.

For a Church embracing ORE, the identity of being co-creators is paramount. The process of co-creation is, of course, highly relational. As the Church, we cannot co-create on our own. That makes no sense. We need a partner to be the "co-" in co-create. We need the guidance of the Spirit in our community to co-create with the triune God. The Spirit has the task of inspiring, calling, and luring us into co-creation. Therefore, the Church must always start with the relationship with God when seeking to co-create.

Oord uses a little story about 9-year-old Gracie to illustrate this need for cooperation:

> Snow fell for two days. When Uncle Johnny, Aunt Kate, and 9-year-old Gracie left the reunion, at least a foot of fluff covered the gym parking lot. As they trudged to the car, relatives helped themselves to second helpings of Thanksgiving pie and watched the Dallas Cowboys on the big screen. Johnny put the Camry in gear and pressed the pedal. It barely moved. The snow was too deep, the incline too steep, and worn tires had little traction. Johnny stepped out to push and Kate slid into the driver's seat. He grunted and strained, calling out advice to Kate and swearing under his breath. Nothing. Little Gracie got out and pushed, but soon gave up. She walked back to the reunion. "Can we get some help out here?" Gracie shouted as she stepped through the gym doors. Within seconds, a half-dozen people grabbed coats and headed outside. Joining Johnny, this quickly formed collective freed the car, and Kate drove onto a clear portion of pavement. A few volunteers laughed at their rapid success. Johnny shook hands and slapped backs, as Kate took a big breath and exhaled her stress. The makeshift crew returned to the Cowboys, and the family of three drove toward home.[15]

This story shows us why we need to co-create. God is like the 9-year-old Gracie. God is not the one who can flick the car up the hill with one mighty push. God is the one who inspires others to use their bodies to help. By inspiring others, the 9-year-old Gracie indeed becomes the most powerful. Gracie is able to move the car

---

15. Oord, *Open and Relational Theology*, 75–76.

because she asks for help and persuades the others to come outside. But had nobody wanted to cooperate, the car would never
have gotten up the hill. In the same way, God is dependent on
our cooperation. God is depending on our will to co-create for
the Basileia to be built.

In this process, the Holy Spirit works as a communicator between what already is and what will be, calling the Church to act
now through a vision of what is to come if we cooperate. For the
Church today to be building the already present Basileia, there
must be a counterpart in the Kingdom that is to come, which
can model and inspire us today. Moltmann notes that "[w]ithout
the counterpart of the kingdom, which transcends the present
system, the transforming power immanent in the system loses its
orientation."[16] There is an orientation in the Basileia to come,
where we need to acknowledge an immanent transforming power
that comes through God's lordship, but that immanent power
always points toward the future Kingdom of God, which transcends this world. In between those two, the Spirit guides the
Church into a cooperative co-creation process. The task in ORE
is working on being a model that signifies the future Kingdom of
God and points toward eschatological hope. This goal, this eschatology, is important to not lose our orientation. And yet we must
remember that we have the power to start building that Kingdom
here and now, to transform our communities to be the Kingdom
of God already now—not like the Kingdom, but to be the actual
immanent Kingdom pointing toward the future transcendent
Kingdom. That is why we co-create creation within creation.

This is an important point for Moltmann: Christianity is not
yet a new creation. Christianity is the cooperative workings of
the Spirit and the Church toward the new creation. Moltmann
notes that "Christianity is not yet the new mankind but it is its

16. Moltmann, *The Church in the Power of the Spirit*, 190.

vanguard, in resistance to deadly introversion and self-giving and representation for man's future."[17] Christianity is, as Moltmann says, the vanguard, trooping forwards to pave the way for all mankind to access the new creation. The Church is to the new creation what John the Baptist was to Christ. The vanguard is making the way, already acting and working, but not yet the full new creation. This view leads to an ultimate openness and an invitation to take part in the creation of the future. It leads to hope and leaves room for the working of the Spirit to cooperate in creating new life and community.

So, why is this so important? Why is the constant focus on cooperation with the Divine important? Often, many ecclesiologies can tend to become more focused on organization and structure. Look, for example, at Dulles's Church as an institution or Church as a sacrament. It can become focused on what Jesus and the apostles said about organizing the Church, how to structure it, how to discern the gifts of the Spirit, and what tools to use in leadership or organizational development. All of these are, of course, great themes and very valuable knowledge. But ecclesiology, in the view of ORT, wants to go further than just structures and leadership.

ORE seeks to redefine what the purpose of the Church is. Ecclesiology is not just a tool to build structures around Christians. In ORE, the purpose of the Church is not to be a structure; it is to be part of eschatological hope for the coming rule of God: to be the image of the Basileia and to constantly work toward building the already present Basileia. ORE is focused, not only on how to organize and structure but also on how we, the Church, take part in God's Mission, the eschatology, and the building of the Kingdom of God already now. ORE must be able to look further than mere structures and instead gaze toward how the Church

---

17. Moltmann, 196.

can cooperate with the Divine. ORE must look more to the Spirit for guidance than toward the world, so to speak. ORE must start by discerning the guidance of the Spirit so it can become the vanguard of mankind, not just another man-made structure.

If we ignore the most basic call of the Church, to work in cooperation with the Spirit to build the Basileia, then ecclesiology becomes solely about hierarchy. Who bears which office, and what functions does that concern? The starting point of ecclesiology cannot be a hierarchy but the acknowledgment that all Christians are members of the messianic people of God and are, in that sense, equals. All Christians, every believer, have an essential contribution to the Kingdom of God because God, through the Spirit, has given each specific gift and task in the building of the Basileia. Ecclesiology is, thus, not about how to organize or structure and who has authority. Ecclesiology is about how the Church and all believers cooperate with the Divine to be co-creators of the Basileia.

There is an important point here: If we lose sight of the eschatological Kingdom of God and if we neglect to cooperate with the Divine through seeking guidance from the Spirit, then our ministry becomes dull and characterless. For the Church to be *in*, but *not of* the world, the overshadowing focus must be seeking guidance from the Spirit. Moltmann reckons that "[t]he ministry is turned an insipid—a 'spiritless'—kind of civil service, and the charisma becomes a cult of the religious genius if we do not make the one charismatically living community our point of departure."[18] For Moltmann, the starting point is the call from the Spirit to each believer to use their gifts in co-creating the new creation within creation. The starting point must be the living community, inspired by the Spirit that seeks to cooperate in co-creating the new creation from within creation itself. If we leave the Spirit out and

---

18. Moltmann, 289–90.

the call to build the Basileia, our Churches will be reduced to mere office-bearers. Ecclesiology is at risk of becoming dead and hierarchical. Without charisma, the Church would be a hollow office building full of bureaucracy. The gifts and inspiration from the Spirit are quintessential for a healthy and living ecclesiology.

So from here, we acknowledge that the theological foundation of ORE rests on these two theological pillars: Firstly, that the Church is called to be in, but not of the world, and secondly, that the Church is called to create the new creation within creation together with the Spirit of the Creator.

From here, we can make this even more practical. Therefore, we can now move on to the three practical outputs of ORE:

- The practical side of co-creating and how we cooperate.
- The need for better, more robust, and more relational leadership built on love.
- The need for unconditional inclusiveness in our communities.

Three Practical Outputs of ORE

There are many aspects I could zoom in on to set up the frame for ORE. I have chosen three practical outputs, which I will use to frame the practical side of ORE.

- The Role of Co-Creators
- The Need for Relational Leadership
- Unconditional Inclusiveness

These are quite distinct aspects of ORE that lead to practices pointing to ORT. These outputs are also distinct in the way that they, to the best of my knowledge, are not commonly embraced in Church life.

I will look more closely at each of these practical outputs in a little while. But before we dive into the specifics, I want to give a short, general overview of these outputs and how they link to ORT so that we have the main ideas clear before moving ahead.

Firstly, ORE builds on the Church's role as a co-creator. It is the job of the Church to already now build the Basileia. God cannot act single-handedly in the world and, therefore, needs partners. The Church has an important job of organizing the hands and feet that God has available and being the resting place where Christians come to be reconnected with God through worship, communion, and teachings. But the focus of the Church is not to build up some grand structure. Instead, the focus is to support, serve, and help the messianic community of God's hands and feet in their everyday life.

Secondly, in ORE, Churches must build their structure around relational leadership. In short, this means that the most important job for a leader is to love and support the people they lead. Leadership must be centered not on authority and hierarchy but on love and true relationships, just like God does not call us to be slaves but to be friends and co-creators. In the same way, God has given humans complete freedom for them to choose to be in a loving relationship with God, our leadership must build on real loving relationships that benefit all parties.

Thirdly, ORE must stand on radical inclusivity. ORT argues for embracing God's radical love, which extends to all people from all walks of life. ORT argues that God wants true loving relationships with all people and wishes to inspire and lure them wherever they are. In the same way, Churches should embrace this radical love in ways of inclusion and by seeking relationships with all of creation.

17.1 The Role as Co-Creators

As stated earlier, God wants creativity to flourish and constantly calls for creation to keep up the process of creation. As humans, we are called to create the already present Basileia. Humans cannot create the Basileia on their own. Creating the Basileia is the task of drawing God's realm into the world as it is right now. This, of course, needs a relational response between Creator and creation through a co-creation process.

In the view of ORT, humanity is the hands and feet of God. Creatures are actually part of the life of God through cooperation. Humans are the creative force that keeps on creating in close cooperation with God. God calls, lures, and coaxes humanity to follow God's plans, but as God does not have a physical localized body, humans must be God's actual hands and feet (see chapters 7.2 and 12).

In this sense, the Christian faith has an inherent call to action. A call to create a realm based on love and empathy, to call out unhealthy power structures and abuse, to care for the wounded, sick, and poor, and to attune creation with the Divine. Essentially, this makes activism an important task for ORE. As the Church is in, but not of the world, the job is to constantly connect to the world more and more to God's being, to the divine love. ORE calls for Churches to embrace and take care of society.

Looking again at Dulles, we can see that the Church is not only the herald that spreads the Good News but also the servant that creates the Good News in the lives of other people. There is also a good connection to Moltmann's Christ-centered ecclesiology. Jesus exactly called us to take care of the ones society had cast out: the sick, the prostitute, and the unwelcome. Jesus dined with sinners to again draw them into the presence of God.[1] This sort of servant attitude is just what is essential to ORE.

Building on ORT, it is important to acknowledge that evil never stems from God and that God does not have any eternal purposes with evil (See chapters 9 and 10.2). One of the main tasks for ORE is to seek out and diminish the evils, sorrows, pains, and other aches of creation. It becomes the role of humanity as co-creators to rid the world of evil in cooperation with the Divine. It becomes the task of ORE to take the responsibility of actualizing the divine possibilities in creating a world based on love.

This is taking seriously that we are in, but not of the world. The Church does not work on the worldly plane but constantly

---

1. Matt. 9:10-17; Mark 2:15-22; Luke 5:29-39.

works to reconnect the world with the Divine and attune creation to the Creator.

The responsibility of being co-creators calls Churches to not be inactive or to shield themselves from the world. It instead calls Churches to live out faith actively and take care of their neighborhood. ORE communities must face what we could call an activist faith. Faith is an activator that sets us on a journey with the vision of healing and rebuilding all of creation, starting with the Church's neighborhood.

Humans are called to live out this activist faith when they realize that evil never stems from God. Gregory Boyd phrases this neatly and says, "When we rid ourselves of any lingering suspicion that evil somehow fits into the eternal purposes of God, we are more inclined to be motivated to do something about it. [...] We are to pray that the Father's will would be done (Matt. 6:10), not accept things as though his will was already being done!"[2] Accepting that evil is never part of God's eternal purpose motivates us to do our Father's will and to actually take part in the divine life. As Boyd says, we pray that the Father's will would be done, not that it is already being done. It is a call to inspire us to act and work toward a better creation. It marks a shift from a passive faith, in which the will is already being done, into an activist faith where we are doing the will of the Father, and the Father inspires and empowers us to this task.

This also touches on another important point for ORE. Spirituality and devotion are not only focused on the inner life but also on seeking God's guidance and help in worldly work. The Christian life should not be focused on a mere strive for happiness and eternal bliss for oneself. It should be a continuing fight for righteousness for all of creation. In this aspect, the spiritual life is

---

2. Boyd, *God of the Possible*, 102.

not something that is purely between God and being, completely separated from the world.

Our spirituality should not only encompass the inner life, but as Moltmann says, "Spirituality includes the whole of life, soul and body, individual and community, the inner life and the outward one."[3] Our spiritual life should be focused on distinguishing what decisions best help us build the Basileia under guidance from the Holy Spirit. This discernment of the guidance of the Spirit is exactly what puts the "co" in "co-creator." It is not "we" who figure out how to best build the Basileia. It is God's guidance that leads us there. We are not just creating or building something here on Earth. We are building what the Master instructs us to. We have our own creative process to put our touch on creation, but God plans, guides, and instructs us humans. We simply step into an ongoing construction process, and by giving our hands to help in the process, we can place our own handprint on our part of creation.

What sets ORE apart is not merely that we create but that we are free to create whatever we want. The Build Master inspires from the point of a greater scheme or blueprint, from which there is a greater overview. But I can choose to listen or do whatever I please. I might even choose to get a wrecking ball and just start destroying everything around me. God does not control my actions due to me being a free being (See Chapter 10: Creation and Freedom). This means that if we choose destructive behavior, we are working against God's plans. Slowing down God and forcing God to redo plans or to even reconstruct earlier creations that have now been torn down due to our destructive behavior. The building of the Basileia, therefore, rests in our hands. If we do not cooperate, it will never happen. God cannot build the Basileia without our cooperation, nor can God force us to cooperate. We

---

3. Moltmann, *The Church in the Power of the Spirit*, 276.

must choose as free beings to either cooperate and build or to work against and be destructive.

The blueprints are in the hands of God. Even though the building process rests in human hands, God's wisdom always works to move the process forward. These blueprints are, of course, working papers that are constantly updated and changed, not one fixed plan for the future. God must be able to change the blueprints to repair eventual damages or destructive behavior and replace it with loving reconciliation. Pinnock emphasizes that "God issues genuine calls for real responses."[4]

As creatures, we are called to give God a real response. Because God does not script our responses and does not control us, God cannot make a complete guide for the entire creation process that will hold from start to finish. Humans often mess up God's plan by either running away, like Jonah or simply turning destructive instead. Therefore, God must have extraordinary wisdom to constantly edit and redo the blueprints and guides so they fit with our responses and can take new actions based on whether we cooperate or not. Pinnock notes that we marvel at God's wisdom, not omniscience, and says, "It is the wisdom of God that we marvel at, not abstract omniscience. Our focus should be on the promises of God, not on his access to a videotaped future."[5] The blueprints hold God's promises but not the complete process with all creaturely actions predestined. Or as Pinnock says it, the future is not videotaped. It is our task, as creatures, to co-create with God to build the Basileia and to build God's promises already in this world.

For Pinnock, the idea of co-creation, or maybe rather that creation of the Basileia depends on us, is key to a practical output of faith: "The fact that God is depending on us is tremendously

---

4. Pinnock, *MOST MOVED MOVER*, 52.

5. Pinnock, 52.

motivating. [...] [God] expects us to be passionately alive; not waiting for the future to happen to us, but intent on creating it with God's help."[6] God calls us to co-create, and therefore, God also expects us to take responsibility for the future, not just wait for the future to happen to us. It is up to us to take the responsibility to build a future based on love, and it is up to us to care for all of creation. And yet God has created us as completely free beings, meaning that God seeks for us to reflect and choose to be part of the co-creation.

This is a very practical aspect of faith that embodies faith as something more than just a mental discipline. God not only stirs and moves something in my core, but the love of God motivates me to reach out with love for my neighbor and to care for the broken and downtrodden. This is what it means to build the Basileia: to live out the rule of God so that communities, people, and creation are called back into the presence of God. It is a practical, hands-on approach to faith. Moltmann notes that "[t]he rule of God is manifested through word and faith, obedience and fellowship, in potentialities grasped, and in free co-operation for the life of the world."[7] This means that the Basileia comes to life where words and faith are manifested through cooperation with God to share God's love with all of creation. The Basileia are utterly dependent on the Church and community of believers to live out God's love. It is the calling of all believers to co-create the Basileia, building on God's inspiration but building with our creaturely hands.

God needs interaction with creatures to drive this creative process. This can be seen as an enormous limitation of God and God's power: that God can only be active if creatures choose to respond. But to this point, Oord is very clear. God has given us

---

6. Pinnock, 168–69.

7. Moltmann, *The Church in the Power of the Spirit*, 192.

ultimate freedom. If not, we could not love and be in real relationships. This freedom also implies that God cannot force us
to act. God can inspire, lure, call, and lead us into God's plans.
Therefore, the creation of the Basileia becomes utterly dependent
on creatures cooperating. That God cannot single-handedly force
my ways does not leave God impotent. The creation of the Basileia
rests upon creaturely forces, factors, and choices.[8] So much is
true. But the creaturely forces, factors, and choices only result in
the building of the Basileia because they are inspired by the wisest and most powerful entity: the God that inspires, equips, and
empowers. In other words, the creative process comes from God,
and Oord says that "God necessarily creates, and God's motive to
create comes from love."[9] This means that in the view of ORT,
God must necessarily create, and we creatures cooperate in that
process. God gives us the power to build the Basileia through
God's love. ORE must have this cooperation as its main activity.

This also means that the community needs to take action! It
is important to remember that we, in the aspect of ORT, make a
real and actual difference in the world with our actions. We affect
people around us, as well as God and God's plans. How we treat
other people, nature, or even other creatures has a real impact on
creation and the Creator. All of our actions have consequences,
both positive and negative. Just as we can be constructive, we,
too, have the power to be destructive. We can choose to cooperate
with God or not. Oord notes that "[t]hose who do not cooperate
with God's loving purposes undermine creation's well-being."[10] If
we do not choose to cooperate with God in building the Basileia
through working toward creating a world and society built on

---

8. Oord, *Pluriform Love: An Open and Relational Theology of Well-Being*, 198.

9. Oord, 198.

10. Oord, *Open and Relational Theology*, 96.

love and good stewardship, then we must be undermining the well-being of creation (See Chapter 10.1: Attunement).

We see this call to cooperation already in Genesis, where God takes the man (Adam) and puts him in the garden of Eden "to tend and keep it."[11] From the get-go, God calls mankind to take care of creation but also to tend to it, cultivate it, and make it flourish. God does not call man to sit back and be mesmerized by the beauty. God calls man to make it even better, to keep creating and co-creating with God. This narrative carries into the NT, where Paul describes how the Holy Spirit gives everyone special gifts that are a "manifestation of the Spirit...given for the common good,"[12] given by God through the Holy Spirit to build up the rule of God, the Basileia. This image is further made clear when Paul next explains that God gives these gifts so that we may be part of the body that is God[13] and that if these gifts are not used out of love, they are misused.[14]

We cooperate with God by using our God-given gifts out of love toward all of creation and toward promoting overall well-being for all of creation.

In this aspect, we move quite beyond Dulles's models. This is what we could call radical servanthood. Greatly simplified, Dulles would argue that the Church, as a servant, is the servant of the world because Jesus calls us to love our neighbor. But ORE argues that the Church becomes the servant because it works to re-attune creation to the Creator. This is done in a close relationship with the Divine, or rather in serving the Divine. That means that the role of servant does not come from discipleship but from the

---

11. Gen. 2:15 (KJV).
12. 1 Cor 12:7
13. 1 Cor 12:12-31
14. 1 Cor 13

call to take part in God's life and own process, and also, the goal is to serve the Creator, not creation.

To take part in this cooperation, we must use the gift that all are given through the Spirit. These gifts, or charisms, are essential to building the Basileia. All are called and inspired to use our specific gifts in the process of creating. To ORE, the participation of all members of the community is essential. God inspires us all to be part of building the Basileia. All are called. All have gifts. This also creates a need for respect between members of the congregation—respect that we all have different gifts and that we should give each other space to unfold our unique gifts as they are given to us by God.

In this aspect, ORE can draw some parallels to the Croatian Protestant theologian and Professor of Theology Miroslav Volf and his participatory ecclesiology. Though Volf probably would not agree with the open aspect of ORT, he weighs in on the relational aspect. In Volf's participatory ecclesiology, he emphasizes the power of laity: that Christ acts through the Gifts that are laid in all of us. For Volf, the Church, in itself, comes into being when people act out their gifts given by the power of the Holy Spirit. Volf writes, "Since [...] all Christians have charisms, Christ also acts through all members of the Church, and not just those who hold office."[15] For Volf, we all participate in the workings of the Church. It is not purely for those who hold offices or are in other ways anointed. The charisms are God's gifts to us that we should use to build the Basileia. They are also a part of God's plans, but God does not force us to use the gifts. They are there resting in us, dormant until we choose to act. This is exactly where the co-creation process of ORE begins: in us activating the charisms we have been given.

---

15. Miroslav Volf, 'A Protestant Response to "We Are the Church: New Congregationalism"', *Concilium*, no. 3 (1996): 39–40.

To put it another way, God gives each of us unique gifts to use in building the Basileia. Christ sets us free to start building, and the Holy Spirit is the power that calls the gifts into life. In ORE, the Spirit holds a special authority in being the messenger. The Spirit is what calls our gifts into life and what gives the community authority. This is what sets the Church apart from other benefactors or philanthropists. The guidance for the work of the Church comes to us from God through the Holy Spirit. The essential difference is that Churches build on the purpose of sharing God's unlimited love with all and responding to the call from God. The Spirit is the source and ground of all the work.

The task of the Church in ORE is to first seek the Spirit in all the work of the Church. This is important because the Church must start by seeking divine inspiration for how and where to work. In this way, the Church allows for the Spirit to call each charism into life. Moltmann neatly phrases it, saying that the Spirit "gives the community the authority for its mission [and] makes living powers and the ministries that spring from them effectively."[16] The Spirit not only calls the gifts into life but also gives each authority to build the Basileia by the gift that is given to each from God. In essence, the Spirit, through the charisms, allows us to live out a little part of the Divine being. In this, the Spirit gives life and power to the ministries. To ORE, the work of the community should always be centered on the power of the Spirit through which God empowers us to co-create.

From the perspective of ORE, charisms are not passive gifts that make the individual able to have a special connection with God. The gifts of the Spirit are given for us to act in the world. To this, Moltmann also notes that the gifts "are not given to us so that we can flee from this world of religious dreams, but [...] intended to witness to the liberating lordship of Christ in this

---

16. Moltmann, *The Church in the Power of the Spirit*, 294.

world's conflicts."[17] In other words, the gifts given to us are intended to show Christ to all of creation, to connect all of creation
to God, and to empower all of creation. To ORE, the main goal
of the charisms is not for us to work ourselves closer to God,
separated entirely from the world around us. The main goal is to
take part in the divine process of continual creation by acting out
God's gifts in this world, thereby building connections for others
to encounter God through us. In ORE, the congregation should
focus more on building up their local community than building
up themselves, so to speak. This is not to neglect ourselves or
to completely give up our well-being to serve others. This focus
builds on sharing God's love. And as Oord defines love, it must
create overall well-being (See Chapter 7.1: ... to promote overall
well-being). This means that if the congregation works to share
God's love, build the Basileia, and focus on building up their local
community, this should have a positive effect on the individual
as well.

God is constantly working to empower creatures to co-create, inspire, and guide creation through the Holy Spirit. As Paul
writes, "There are different kinds of working, but in all of them
and everyone it is the same God at work."[18] God gives us these
gifts out of grace so that we might be creative partners for God.
The gifts are, so to speak, the energies of the new life—the energy
to be a co-creator of the Basileia. The gifts lead us to co-create the
new creation along with our community and the entire body of
Christ. When we join in the co-creative act, we honor and serve
God. Moltmann says, "Creative grace leads to new obedience;
and the gifts of grace and the energies of the Spirit lead to ready,
courteous service. Claims and privileges cannot be deduced from

---

17. Jürgen Moltmann, *The Spirit of Life: A Universal Affirmation* (Minneapolis: Fortress Press, 2001), 186.

18. 1 Cor. 12:6

them. The source of life's new forces in the new life itself."[19] This new life energy flows from God through the Spirit, as a call to co-create and use the gifts that we have been given. The call to be co-creators comes with authority and the power to act, as well as the charisms as tools to use in building the Basileia.

To try to sum up this point, in ORE, our greatest call is to be co-creators. God calls us to co-create the Basileia together with the Creator. This means to make the ruling of God visible on earth right now. God needs partners who are free and willing co-creators to extend God's rule to all of the earth. The act of building the Basileia cannot be done solely from inside the Church building. The call to co-create is, therefore, also a call to act and meddle in the world we see around us. It is a call for the congregation to act in their local community in whatever way possible to show the loving rule of God. ORE argues that the charisms, the gifts of the Spirit, are given to us to build the Basileia. When we use these gifts and let us be inspired by God, we become active partners, active co-creators in the divine process. In ORE, the call to co-create the Basileia is the main goal. God created humans to be free and active agents in this world to take care of and tend to creation. Not only are we called to take care of creation but also to work with it, evolve it, and bring it closer to God's grace. A congregation embracing ORE cannot be a passive one. It must work for the best of its community, both those who are part of the congregation and those who live in the vicinity. The call to co-create and build the Basileia is the highest honor and cornerstone of ORE.

This cornerstone brings with it two other practical aspects: the need for relational leadership, which will help us build the Basileia within our community, and a call for radical inclusiveness, which will help us build the Basileia in the community around us.

---

19. Moltmann, *The Church in the Power of the Spirit*, 295.

17.2 The Need for Relational Leadership

ORE stands firm on the call of the Church communities to be part of building the Basileia in a continuing co-creation process with God. Now, this also has implications for how we build the Church community. For good reasons, it is hard to build a community and run an organization without any leadership. We must organize, lead, and work with people to build a good, robust, and healthy community. But this then raises the question: What would be an effective and robust way to build leadership in the eyes of ORE?

To answer this, we must start, naturally, with the basis of ORT. The firm grounding of ORT is the basic notion that God's essence is love and that God, more than anything, seeks true, authentic relationships with creatures. From that, we can deduce that there is something good about relationships. And more than that, there is something divine about relationships. ORT teaches us that there is a divine nature and admirable character in the structure of true and authentic relationships. Since God has unending love toward all people, so should we lead from the point of loving our neighbor.

Placing relationships in the center of leadership becomes important because every person has endless value and worth in the identity of God's beloved child. Every person is made in the image of the Creator and is loved by the Creator. Therefore, leadership must never work to reduce another person. It must always build on love and true relationships with another person. Relational leadership will always seek to enhance every person because each person is endlessly valuable. And in ORT, each person has an endless value because each is created by a loving Creator and carries the image of God.

So, what might leadership look like if we placed the relation to the other at the center? This chapter will give a short introduction to relational leadership and, from that, discuss the benefits of relational leadership to ORE.

To give a perspective on relational leadership, we can start by looking at the antithesis of relational leadership; here, I am thinking of the very popular management tool Lean. The goal of Lean is to optimize the value stream, meaning to make sure the company only pays for things that are of value to the customer.[20] Therefore, Lean needs to, as much as possible, reduce each person into an abstract value based on their importance and value to the bottom line. This is, of course, a generalization and oversimplification, but it encapsulates the essence. Tools like Lean try to reduce people to mere numbers and abstract values so that they can be moved around in a spreadsheet and, if they do not make enough profit, be sacked to make the organization more efficient and create higher earnings for the investors and better prices for the customers. It makes sense that Lean has its raison d'être in manufacturing. On an assembly line, there is no need for workers who are not of direct importance to the product that comes out the other end.[21] This thinking makes sense in a factory setting but is certainly hard to combine with a Church setting, yet there are, unfortunately, some that try.

As I have said, the Lean model is as close to the sole antithesis of relational leadership as can be. In many ways, the Lean model seeks to reduce, or at least simplify, the worth and value of people to their ability to make money. In the exact opposite way, relational leadership seeks to respect the intrinsic and endless value of all people. A person is not only valued if they are able to make

---

20. Sheila Benah and Yang Li, 'Examining the Relationship between Lean Supplier Relationship Management (LSRM) and Firm Performance: A Study on Manufacturing Companies in Ghana', *Open Journal of Business and Management* 08, no. 06 (2020): 2423–50, https://doi.org/10.4236/ojbm.2020.86150.

21. Simon Caulkin, 'Britain's Best Factories', *Management Today*, no. November (1990): 60–89.

money for the investors. A person is of value because he or she is created by God in the image of the Creator. Relational leadership looks to benefit the person first to build robust and capable people instead of just looking toward their output.

Therefore, the question of robust relational leadership becomes: How do we lead people in our community in a respectable and loving way that seeks to enhance the individual person?

In ORE, the Church should become countercultural to Lean and work to build its leadership on the Christian deeds of empathy, love, relations, and caring. In my eyes, these are deeds that have more or less been ruled out of contemporary leadership theories, as they are not easily calculable or profitable. In a world where we are measured and weighed on every action we take, the Church should become the place where a person is worthy simply because they are created by God. Simply by being created, a person is worthy of love, respect, and empathy, no matter what.

This calls for Churches to place the single person and the relation between the leader and that person, as the absolute centerpiece. In ORE, all influence of another person must naturally be directed toward the good of the person and their relationship with their leaders and overall well-being. All influence must be exerted to enhance the overall well-being of the individual and the organization.

So how do we, as Church leaders, lead through the relation, and in what ways does ORE benefit from focusing on relational leadership? At the outset, we will look at how to practically work with "relational leadership." The issue here is that no one has trademarked relational leadership. Lean is much easier to define, as big management companies have trademarked and written many explanations about it. Relational leadership is not completely undefined, but it is, in many ways, an outsider in contemporary leadership thinking. In this book, I will give a short overview of the core values of relational leadership as it is most often described and, after that, examine the theology of relational leadership.

Relational leadership builds on five core values: Purpose, Inclusive, Empowering, Ethical, and Process.[22] The following short introduction is built on Susan Komives' introduction to relational leadership. I will be using the word employee here to denote the objects of a leader's actions. We do not often talk about employees in Church literature, but whether we lead a hired employee or a member of our congregation, the power of leadership works in the same way. So, for now, bear with the word "employee." The five core values are as follows:

> **Purpose:** The relational leader needs to point the employee toward a clear purpose that can be articulated. This is important because it creates an aim for the organization and the individual. There is an actual end in sight that we are working toward together, and we can aim for it together. This is important to create an aim and goal for the success of the work being done.

> **Inclusion:** The relational leader needs to build a culture of inclusiveness. This is done by making sure to value everyone's experience and opinion. It does not mean that we should be accepting or blindly following everyone's opinions. The leader must still make the final decision and steer toward the purpose, all the while listening intently to everyone and carefully weighing their perspectives. It is important to make sure everyone experiences that they are being seen.

---

22. Susan R. Komives, *Exploring Leadership: For College Students Who Want to Make a Difference*, Third edition (San Francisco: Jossey-Bass, 2013).

Empowerment: The relational leader must empower all employees to bring out the best in all. The relational leader must be aware of the strengths and weaknesses of the team. From there, the leader can work to bring forth the strengths and help to improve the weaknesses. For the relational leader, individual growth leads to organizational growth. This takes time and effort and demands building a close and trusting connection with the employee. Weaknesses become potential for development.

Ethical: The relational leader must, of course, work in an ethical way. Ethics is of utmost importance. The leader works with people's lives and must, therefore, be respectable, value everyone, and never diminish, exploit, or hurt an employee. The ethical, relational leader must also set a good example to embody the organization's values.

Process: Last, but definitely not least, the relational leader must value the process. The process is the basis of great relational leadership. The focus must be to encourage reflection, collaboration, independence, and creativity. This includes the risk of letting go of the handle and not being able to control every action but trusting the employees. [23]

The relational leader seeks to lead with purpose through inclusiveness, empowerment, and ethics, all the while respecting the process. And looking at this from the perspective of the Church, we should add a sixth bullet point: The leader must be **open toward the other**. This means being open to influence and to being influenced by the other in the relationship. When the leader shows love in a relational response to God and the other, this also

---

23. Komives.

has a transformative effect, where the two sides of the relationship build up and shape eachother.

Throughout this chapter, I will explore how and in what ways ORE can benefit from relational leadership and why this might be a great match for the theology of ORE.

First of all, we must acknowledge that in all relationships, we are open to the other person, and we let that person influence us. There is, so to speak, a flow of power between the parts of the relationship. There is an influence between the parts of the relationship. This is true whether we talk about the relationship with another person or God. There will always be an influence both ways. (See Chapter 8: God needs to be responsive to truly love.)

In a relational frame of mind, we can define power as the ability to influence. The more I can influence another person, the more power I have over them. I can influence other people or things in compassionate, benign ways or evil, destructive ways. Whatever it may be, there will always be an influence both ways in a relationship. Keller notes that "[w]ithin a relationship, the power flow is never altogether unilateral, however asymmetrical it may be."[24] By this, Keller says that power goes both ways. We are influenced by the other while influencing. This power structure may not be symmetrical. For example, the power structure between humans and God surely is not symmetrical at all but is neither altogether unilateral, meaning that it is not a completely one-way action. Of course, human's power to influence God is way smaller than the reverse action. Still, humans change God through our relationship. In human relationships, the power structure is never symmetrical, either. In the Church, there will always be some that have more power, either through structure or seniority. This only makes it more important for us to be sensitive to the power structures and work constructively through the relationship.

---

24. Keller, *On the Mystery*, 80.

Acknowledging that we influence as much as we are being influenced ourselves is essential. Relational leadership is key to ORE, as it teaches us to lead in the same fashion as we see God lead in scripture. God leads us through affection. God is affected by creatures, and through that affection, affects back. In the same way, we should build our understanding of leadership in ORE.

The American professor and process theologian Bernhard Loomer worked to define relational power as opposed to purely unilateral power. For Loomer, unilateral power creates obstructive and impoverishing structures of injustice by highlighting natural and cultivated inequalities.[25] As the counterweight to this, relational power works to use the natural and cultivated inequalities to help each other forward. Loomer does not try to hide that there are natural inequalities in our society. Loomer instead argues that relational power builds on squeezing good from these inequalities. For example, one Church leader may come from a middle-class home and has been able to study in Denmark, where education is free. If this leader comes to an American Church, where the leader meets a young woman from a poor community who has an ambition and motivation to become the leader of tomorrow, then the first leader can back her up, help her fundraise, and become a mentor to her. In that way, the first leader uses the inherent inequality and the leader's advantages to help the leader of tomorrow. In that way, the Church leader shares the surplus of the inequality with the new leader. This means working to share power, influence, economy, and other such means.

This is, of course, a very caricatured example just to show the point. The relational power may be even more relevant when we look at day-to-day examples. If one employee is stressed, the leader can either use the higher influence of his or her position to get the employee more time off. Or for a while, the leader can step

---

25. Loomer, 'Two Conceptions of Power'.

in and help with some of the tasks of the employee because the leader has more time. It might be as simple as a humble "How are you today?" Anyway, these small everyday examples show us how relational power comes in terms of serving and lifting the other person instead of diminishing the other.

Looking back to Dulles, this again shows us that ORE fits into the category of the Church as a servant. But more so, this structure also sits well with what Jesus taught us about leadership. In Matt. 20:16, Jesus insists that the last will be first, and the first will be last. And then he goes on to say that "whoever wants to become great among you must be your servant, and whoever wants to be first must be your slave."[26] For Jesus, authority and leadership are linked with servanthood. For Jesus, leadership is done through relationships by humbly adjusting to serve your congregation or employees. There is an inherent relational power that is only owned through servanthood.

Serving another means to enhance the other's very being. To this, Loomer writes that "it is the hope that in the practice of relational power, we may learn how to interrelate these inequalities so they may become mutually enhancing."[27] For Loomer, unilateral power leads to injustice through cultivating our inequalities. The strong get stronger, and the weak get weaker. Relational power sees, according to Loomer, inequalities as strengths that mutually will enhance both parties of the relationship and as opportunities to serve and love our neighbor.

We see this in Jesus' way of addressing God as Abba, as a father,[28] and in saying, "Truly I tell you, anyone who will not receive the kingdom of God as a little child will never enter it."[29] God uses

---

26. Matt. 20:26-27
27. Loomer.
28. Mark 14:36
29. Mark 10:15

the inequality of the relationship to enhance both parts. We come to God as children, without expectations of certain performance and without having to live up to any rules or regulations, and God blesses us with an excess of love as only a parent can. This is an example to be followed by leaders: to steward their power and unequal position to lift employees. It is inspirational for the way we look at leadership in ORE. As leaders, we will often be in a higher position than those we lead. This means we have the ability and obligation to serve those we lead with love and respect. As leaders, we are called to be servants of those we lead. Jesus tells us that "[t]he greatest among you will be your servant" and that those you will humble themselves shall be exalted.[30] Jesus' way of leading is the way of serving. It is the relational approach, where leadership springs from robust relationships.

Serving others is the special power of relational leadership. Mesle includes three important practical steps in building relational leadership. These are built on how we see God use relational power in scripture.[31]

1) The relational leader must first gain the ability to actively be open to the world around them and let themselves be affected by the world and people around them.

2) The relational leader must then take in these experiences and affections. From that, they must let themselves be created and formed by affection.

3) The relational leader must lastly use them to influence back on those around them, having first been affected by them.[32]

---

30. Matt. 23:11-12

31. Mesle, *Process-Relational Philosophy*.

32. Mesle, 73.

These three steps show us that relational power is always a reaction to affection. As we are created to be in true relationships with each other and built on love, we should work toward affecting each other positively.

Mesle bases his three steps on the work of Bernard Loomer, who was one of the early contributors to process theology. Loomer furthermore argues that human power is analogous to God's power, as both are active through the relational response between two entities. Interestingly, Loomer infers that our power must be analogous to God's, just like Oord infers that our love must be analogous to God's. In other words, human power works in the same way that God's power works in the world. Mesle, therefore, seeks to mold his view on relational power from the way we see God act and use relational power in scripture. This leads to a view where we are open to and affected by the people around us with whom we are in relation. Their experiences, thoughts, hopes, sorrows, etc., affect and change us. We create ourselves from what we have taken in from the other person, so to speak. From that point, we can influence those around us, not because we have some sort of greater power from the outside, but because they have affected us first.[33]

In Loomer's perspective, the aim of power from a relational point of view is not to control or coerce another person. It is not to use the relation to manipulate another human being. Loomer states that "[t]he greatest possible good cannot emerge under conditions of control. The aim is to provide those conditions of the giving and receiving of influences such that there is the enlargement of the freedom of all the members to both give and receive."[34] Relational power should aim to enlarge the freedom of both parties in the relationship. To Loomer, the greatest possible

---

33. Loomer, 'Two Conceptions of Power'.

34. Loomer.

good can only emerge from the enlarged freedom that relational power induces. The relationship and the power that flows between us create both of us. It sets us free to be a greater version of ourselves. In that sense, the relationship is not about committing to each other, but rather committing to a relational "us."

To ORE, this means that leadership should always be from the perspective of relational power. As leaders of a congregation, we do not seek to control or coerce the output of another person's life or choices. Relational leadership means to enlarge the freedom of both the one giving and the one receiving affection. We can never control another's actions, but we can commit to a relational "us," where we, in cooperation, move forward.

To Loomer, there is also an interdependency between giving and receiving, influencing and being influenced, etc. These are all interwoven, as in there is not one that gives and one that receives, but both parties of a relationship constantly give and receive. Loomer writes, "At times they seem to be almost indistinguishable and their roles appear to be interchangeable. Often the greatest influence that one can exercise on another consists of being influenced by the other, in enabling the other to make the largest impact on one's self."[35]

Relational leadership is a process of allowing the other to influence me and in return influence the other back. These aspects become indistinguishable and a constant process of influencing each other. This movement back and forth helps us to build empathy for the other person. When we are affected by the other, we start to see the world through their eyes, which enables us to understand their point of view. In relational leadership, we need empathy to understand the other and to act intentionally and lovingly to promote overall well-being and to enlarge the freedom of all parties.

---

35. Loomer.

Jesus teaches his followers to "Do to others as you would have them do to you."[36] This Golden Rule is the very foundation of relational leadership. We must stop and ask: *How would I like to be treated in a similar situation? What would enhance the over-all well-being in this situation?* And then choose a path to move forward.

Relational leadership becomes important in ORE as it builds on loving our neighbor and seeing the infinite value of all persons. This is the love that God created us to live out (See Chapter 7: It all starts with Love). The relational character is constituted by God and is therefore an example to be followed by us. It also holds true for the open character of God. As God does not coerce us, we should not coerce each other. God's exemplary style of leading us is through inspiring, calling, and challenging. This is always done in a true relationship. We should strive to lead in the same manner.

In a relationship, there is also a mutual creation of each other. Loomer leans a lot on the philosophical movement "personalism" in his view of relational leadership. I will not do a deep examina-tion of personalism in this book, but just note that personalism states that every human is relational, worthy, involved, and con-sists of both nature and spirit.[37] One of the main thinkers behind personalism was the Austrian philosopher Martin Buber, who wrote a thought-provoking little book called *I and Thou*. Buber's project was to show that all humans create each other in the truly loving and enquiring meeting between an I and a Thou. When we do not hold the other person accountable for our preconceptions but truly investigate their being and are curious about what we find in the other person, that is where we find true empathy, and

---

36. Luke 6:31

37. Jonas Mortensen, *Det fælles bedste: introduktion til personalismen*, ed. Steffen Boeskov and Leif E. Kristensen, 1. udgave, 1. oplag (Frederiksværk: Boedal, 2012).

that is where we create a part of each other's being. Buber writes. "Love is the responsibility of an I for a Thou: in this consists what cannot consist in any feeling—the equality of all lovers."[38] To Buber, the true meaning of love in the relationship is the caring responsibility that we create as a part of the other person in the true meeting.

Now, why is this bit of background information about personalism important? When we are working with relational leadership, we are not just taking care of business, so to speak. The goal is not mainly to manage an organization for profit and show value to the investors. The main goal of relational leadership is to take responsibility for our neighbor, for those we work with and do Church with, and to take responsibility for their growth and flourishing. Relational leadership seeks to build up the other person and, in doing so, also builds up the organization.

Again, Loomer writes that "[t]he knowing and the being known are mutually creative. Presence means that both knowing and being known are functions of the creativity of both the speaking and the listening."[39] For Loomer, the relational power resonates clearly with the wording of Buber's *I and Thou*. We are creating each other in and through the relationship. We create each other in speaking, as well as listening.

Jesus also taught us to think this way about leadership and wield power in this fashion. Jesus showed his authority by washing the feet of his disciples.[40] In scripture, it says that when he had finished washing their feet, Jesus asked them: "Do you understand what I have done for you?"[41] and they do not. So, Jesus goes on and tells them that when he, as their Lord and Teacher,

---

38. Martin Buber, *I and Thou*, 46. print., 1. Touchstone ed, A Touchstone Book (New York: Simon & Schuster, 1996).

39. Loomer, 'Two Conceptions of Power'.

40. John 13

41. John 13:12

has washed their feet, they should do the same to one another: "Very truly I tell you, no servant is greater than his master, nor is a messenger greater than the one who sent him."[42] John Sanders notes that in this very action, Jesus redefines what it means to be a leader and to wield power.[43] It is by empathically serving through love that we wield power correctly. In the same way, Jesus tells his disciples that the greatest of them is the one that serves the others.[44] To Jesus, leadership is not about power and influence. It is about serving, loving, and building up the people we have responsibility for.

The same is true for relational leadership, which is why it is so important for ORE. The goal is not power, influence, or money. The goal of relational leadership is servitude, affection, and love. Through relational leadership, the leader takes part in creating the people around them, just as the people around the leader create the leader. Similarly, humans are affected and created in their relationship with God, and vice versa. Relational leadership takes seriously the open aspect of creation and seeks to lead in the same relational way that God shows us, and that is lived out in Jesus Christ. The goal of relational leadership is to steward and care for the people around us and, through that caring, create movement that moves the entire organization forward in a way that makes everyone grow.

So to sum up, we are looking at the three practical aspects of ORE. Firstly, we must seek inspiration from God to take part in the co-creation process. And secondly, this process flows into our leadership, which must be built on relational power, stewardship,

---

42. John 13:16

43. John Sanders, *Embracing Prodigals: Overcoming Authoritative Religion by Embodying Jesus' Nurturing Grace* (Eugene, OR: Cascade Books, 2020), 23.

44. Luke 22:24-27

and empathy. This leads us to the last practical aspect: that ORE must live out radical inclusiveness toward all of creation.

17.3 Radical Inclusiveness

The third and final aspect of ORE is the call to radical inclusiveness. Because God created all in God's own picture, everybody is infinitely valuable and a part of creation. Everyone is God's beloved child, and in ORE, we must meet all people as a brother or sister in the beloved family of God's children. A Church embracing ORE must be open and inclusive toward God, creation, and the future. Being open to all of creation means being open and inclusive toward all human beings, no matter their background, religion, political stance, or other factors. And it also means to be open and inclusive toward the rest of creation: nature, environment, animal life, etc. This is the radical inclusiveness of ORE.

Radical in this context means that the Church must be welcoming all unconditionally to the community of the Church, just like God wants real and true relationships with all, no matter where they are in their journey.

Looking back to Chapter 8.1: Panentheism, I explained that ORT looks at the connection between Creator and creation as a panentheistic connection, where God is immanent *in* all of creation. And in Chapter 9, I laid out the essence/experience binate that God has an everlasting, unchanging essence (love), while God's experience changes with creation (process). Why is this important? The call to radical inclusiveness arises in just these two points. God is immanent through all creatures and experiences all creatures as part of the process. All humans have endless value, as all humans are exactly created in the image of God, and God wants relationships with all.

It is important to set this record straight from the get-go! That God is immanent through all of creation means that, as Oord phrases it, "We are in God's experience, but not identical to God."[45] That God is immanent in all of creation does not mean that all of creation is God. It means that we are deeply connected to God through a loving relationship. Jesus says, "Truly I tell you, whatever you did for one of the least of these brothers and sisters of mine, you did for me."[46] Whatever we do to the least of God's beloved children, whatever we do to nature, and whatever we do to any part of creation, we do to God. Therefore, we must be loving and welcoming toward all and be in service to all around us, whether it is a person or the environment.

As a community and as ORE, we too are connected with the love of God; we are obliged to love as God would and invite all into this loving relationship. God already loves every creature endlessly, as all are in God's experience. So must we.

When ORT states that God formed us in God's own image, there is also a practical aspect that leads us to a place of duality. By this, I mean that ORT states that all are created in God's ultimate love, but it is a job left to us to embrace this love and let us be formed by it. God does not, and cannot, force us to love. Sanders makes the important note that our view of God has a great power to produce our personality. If we see God as a strong and tribal deity, we want to build fences, yet if we see God as nurturant, empathetic, forgiving, and loving, we will meet people with that same attitude. Sanders writes, "Our Gods make us in their image because we imitate the God we believe in."[47] Or to expand it a bit, when embracing ORT, God is seen as ultimate love and thus creates us with the ability to embrace ultimate love, but we must do the act of loving ourselves.

---

45. Oord, *Open and Relational Theology*, 103.

46. Matt. 25:40

47. Sanders, *Embracing Prodigals*, 40.

When we embrace the other person, we are in a process with God. As God is immanent in all of creation and is seeking true and real relationships with all of creation, we are cooperating in the process when we create open and welcoming spaces by opening up, welcoming others, and embracing them into our midst, not that they may assimilate to our ways, but that they may help us to develop and that we may help them to become more closely connected to God.

To explore this aspect of radical inclusiveness, we shall look mainly toward Moltmann, who makes the point that discipleship is the Basileia that already is present. I will, of course, bring in other thinkers to give some perspective to this.

What is important for Moltmann is that conservatism is seen as counterproductive to God's work. As God is in an everlasting process, always moving forward and creating, conservatism would be counterproductive to the divine process. This does not mean, though, that we, as a Christian society, cannot have some fundamental beliefs. It means that creation, society, and culture are always in the process of moving forward. This is divine, and we must work to discern Christ and God in that process. If we chose conservatism, we chose to step out of that process and work against the process of God. The task for Church communities is to always translate the fundamental beliefs to the next generation in the language of—and appropriate to the culture of—the next generation and, in that way, be inclusive to all people and movements in culture.

A closed and introverted community, thus, has no future because it has no process. The community of Christians must embrace an open and inclusive attitude toward the surrounding society to make Christ understandable and tangible. This visionary and prophetic task of making Christ understandable to a new generation is indeed difficult and perilous. It is a task that creates much friction, and the idea of opening up toward a new generation can be frightening for conservative communities. The first who try to progress and develop new language and understanding can often find themselves being excluded or pushed away from their own communities. To this Moltmann notes that "[w]ithout the price of this perilous openness to the world and time, there is no future, no freedom, and no life for people or human society. For what closes itself within itself is condemned to death and has a deadly effect on other life."[48] For Moltmann, conservatism and closed structures are deadly to communities. Closed communities can have no hope for the future and will, therefore, wind up as dead entities. Only in a hopeful and inclusive openness toward the work can Church life thrive.

As to this, it is important to also note that to Moltmann, the Church is a relational structure, not only for those within the community but also for the community as a whole. Moltmann says that "[t]he Church cannot understand itself alone. It can only truly comprehend its mission, meaning, roles, and functions in relation to others."[49] And by "others," Moltmann refers to the culture of the surrounding society. This means that the community of the Church cannot comprehend its meaning and mission on its own. It needs to be in a relational response toward the surrounding culture, as well as God. The Church is, so to speak, stretched out between God and the people, who God wants to meet. Therefore, it is counterproductive for the Church to close itself off from the world and "conserve" itself. It must be open and, with love and inclusivity, invite the surrounding society to take part in the life of God as well.

To Moltmann, this means that ecclesiology must be open in three dimensions. Ecclesiology must be open before God, before creation, and before the future. Moltmann says that "[t]he

---

48. Moltmann, 194.
49. Moltmann, 19.

Church atrophies when it surrenders any one of these openness's and closes itself up against God, men or the future."[50] These three legs of openness—being open toward God, humans, and the future—are all vital to keeping the Church up to its task. If one falls away, the Church will stumble and fall. If we are closed off from God, well, there is not much Christianity then. We are no longer guided in the process by the Divine. If we close off humans, then we miss the call to bring all people before God. And if we close off the future, then we close off all the eschatological hope for creation. This is also what Karl Barth defines by saying that the Church "has always needed, and it always will need, self-examination and self-correction. It cannot exist except as *ecclesia semper reformanda.*"[51] The Church must always reform itself to keep being present, healthy, and working, or it will falter.

The continuing reformation of the Church is important to keep being in a relational response to God and others. As said, love carries a dimension of relational response. If we do not keep reforming, we do not act on God's relational response. More than that, God is always present in and through all of creation. This is what is meant by God's omnipresence in a panentheistic frame. God is present to us and all of our neighbors, co-workers, friends, and all the rest of creation. When God is always present to all humans and all of creation, this means that what we do in relational response to others affects God. As Oord states, we, consequently, "promote the well-being of an omnipresent, relational God when we promote the well-being of neighbours, ourselves, and creation."[52] Opening our communities with radical inclusiveness and meeting everyone with love and caring is a relational response to God's lures.

---

50. Moltmann, 2.

51. Karl Barth, *Church Dogmatics, Volume IV, The Doctrine of Reconciliation* (Edinburgh: T & T Clark, 1956), 690.

52. Oord, *Pluriform Love: An Open and Relational Theology of Well-Being*, 104.

The task of the Church then becomes to start creating the coming glory and peace of the Kingdom, the Basileia. This can be done through discipling Christ, working for greater love and freedom for all of creation, and working against oppression and division. Moltmann even takes this one step further, saying, "The coming peace of the kingdom will be lived in the discipleship of Christ and mutual service for freedom."[53] This means that when we work actively for greater freedom and love and when we live in the discipleship of Jesus Christ, we partake in the Basileia right now. The call for radical inclusiveness through love and freedom is, to Moltmann, the sign of the Basileia that already is.

As disciples of Christ, we are also shown how Jesus works with radical inclusiveness to again, attune creation to God. Jesus seeks the company of sinners, prostitutes, and tax collectors to once again attune them to God. This example of being the doctor or healer to the sick and not the healthy[54] is what Jesus shows us to do.

As to this point, the Basileia cannot be seen as a purely religious kingdom, meaning that it cannot simply be realized through a new religion, as Christianity has become. A part of the Basileia is seen now, through the power of our religion and morality as disciples of Christ, but there is also an all-important eschatological aspect. Moltmann writes that "[t]he eschatological reign of God, whom Jesus as Kyrios represents and whose power he exercises, cannot, therefore, be limited. It bursts the bonds of a divided world."[55] Moltmann reckons that the reign of God, the Basileia, embraces and includes all of creation. All of what is in creation is in relational response to the Creator; therefore, all must be included. The Basileia works against a divided world. To this, the communities of Christians in the Church should be forebearers.

---

53. Moltmann, *The Church in the Power of the Spirit*, 292.

54. Mark 2:17

55. Moltmann, 100.

The Church must, therefore, seek to be a free and open fellowship of equal friends where there is room for all and all are included. In ORE, the Church embraces people from all walks of life and helps them all to move toward the cross, toward Christ. For Moltmann, this fellowship mimics the relationship of the Trinity. Or in other words, the fellowships of the Church should mirror the egalitarian relationship of the Trinity,[56] a structure where all bring different gifts to the table and all are welcomed. ORE must embrace radical inclusiveness, where all are equal in their attempt to follow Christ in discipleship.

The inclusiveness of the community also points to Jesus' way of calling his disciples: "Follow me."[57] He simply prompts people to follow. Christ does not demand anything else from people other than them following him. The fellowship of our Church is modeled on Christ's example: an unconditional and prevenient invitation. Moltmann notes that "[i]t [the fellowship of the Church] cannot limit Christ's invitation on its own account. Everyone who wants to participate can participate in the fellowship of Christ. The communion is an answer to Christ's open invitation."[58] Moltmann points to Christ's own unconditional invitation for everyone to follow in an open fellowship. Jesus called the sinners to follow. In the same way, the community of ORE must be open and unconditionally inviting to people from all walks of life to be part of the process. We cannot limit the invitation to our own accord.

To try and round off this chapter on the radical inclusiveness prompted in ORE. To begin with, ORT acknowledges that God is in an everlasting process of creating. This is done in a relational

---

56. Veli-Matti Kärkkäinen, *Introduction to Ecclesiology: Ecumenical, Historical & Global Perspectives* (Downers Grove, Ill: InterVarsity Press, 2002), 128.

57. Matt. 4:19

58. Moltmann, *The Church in the Power of the Spirit*, 259.

response with all of creation. As Christians, we should partake in the process and help to develop the future of faith communities. For all this to be possible, we must seek to be open before the dimension of God, of humans, and the future. A conservatism will directly counteract God's process of creation. Instead, we must seek to always make God and salvation through Christ tangible and understandable for new generations. This process requires progressivism. But more important than that, it requires unconditional radical inclusiveness for all people to follow and join in the process, just like Jesus showed us. Radical inclusiveness is essential for the development of ORE.

For our community to practically embrace ORE, these last three points show us that, firstly, we must seek inspiration from God to take part in the co-creation process. Secondly, this process flows into our leadership, which must be built on relational power, stewardship, and empathy. And thirdly, the process of co-creating and the call to relational power brings with it a need for radical inclusiveness toward all of creation so that all can come to God as beloved children.

17.4   Then what defines Open and Relational Ecclesiology?

In this chapter, I will sum up what defines ORE and try to forge a path that we can follow to explore ORE further. This book is just a beginning. This is only an inkling pointing toward ORE. The open and relational community still has much work to further explore and deepen the understanding of ORE. For now, we have begun a journey that will let us explore this field event further.

In Figure 1 below, I have tried to create an infographic that gives an overview of the five steps on the way to building the Basileia, in other words, to practically work toward ORE.

Overall, the framework for ORE is to create the already present Basileia. God works toward the Basileia to come. The blueprints are not complete as the future is not settled. God constantly adjusts and re-adjusts the plans according to how well creation cooperates with God. It is our task to be attuned to God and act in the co-creation process.

For the Church, this leads us to two theological observations: steps one and two on the infographic.

Firstly, the Church is called to be in, but not of the world. This means that the Church is called to establish the already present realm of divine ruling, the Basileia, here in the world. This is a realm that is countercultural to the present day's worldly structures. The Basileia builds on the divine essence, on love, and on creating overall well-being. This step takes seriously the open aspect of ORT. We are called to cooperate with the Divine and act on the call and inspiration of God. We can choose whether we want to cooperate with the Divine or not. And secondly, the Church is placed in a continual process of co-creation. This step takes seriously the relational aspect of ORT. God wants and needs true relationships with all of creation. These relationships are essential to the continual creation process of the Basileia.

These two theological observations carry with them three practical outputs of how we may structure our communities (steps three to five). The third step mainly concerns the nature of the Church, whereas steps four and five are practical, necessary tasks for the Church.

Thirdly, the Church must practice the role of co-creator. This means that the community must actively be working toward building the Basileia. The call of the Church is not only to gather and worship but to follow in the footsteps of Jesus, bringing healing to the broken and the sick, standing up against injustice, caring for creation, and dining with sinners and prostitutes. In short, the nature of the Church must be to actively try to live as Jesus Christ showed us.

Figure 1 The 5 steps toward building the Basileia.
This encapsulates Open and Relational Ecclesiology

5 steps on the way to be building
THE BASILEIA

1

In, but not of the world

The church is called to establish the realm of divine ruling already now, and to re-attune beings to God, so that all of creation can one day cooperate with God.

2

The process of continual co-creation

God is constantly working to create the basileia. The church is called to take part in this process and co-create creation together with the Creator

3

The Role as Co-creator

In practice this means, that our actions affect God and the future. God will always call, lure, and inspire us, but we must choose whether we cooperate or not.

4

A need for relational leadership

Our leadership must be build on love and respect for the other. Like God leads us through the true loving relationship, so must we build our local leadership

5

Radical Inclusiveness

God is immanent in all of creation and more than that wishes a real relationship with all creatures. Our communities must embrace all people to help them on in their process with the divine

Fourthly, there is a need for relational leadership. This means that our ways of leading people in the organization must be formed by how God leads creatures. Therefore, leadership must be loving, meaning that leadership works to enhance overall well-being. Our ways of leading must recognize the endless value of each person in our organization and work with love and respect for the individual.

Fifthly, the Church must work toward radical inclusiveness. As God is immanent in all of creation and wants a true relationship with every creature, so must the community of the Church work to include all people from all walks of life in the organization. Every person has endless value because God is panentheistically immanent in every person. Furthermore, every person is in their own process with God and their own relationship with God.

As an organization, we must support that and work to help the person with his or her process.

These five steps in building the Basileia encapsulate the way toward ORE. As I stated in my introduction to ecclesiology, the difficult part of working with ecclesiologies is that it draws strings to all of the other -ologies of our theology. So, there are still many unexplored parts of ORE, for example, how eschatology or soteriology connects with ecclesiology. This is only the start of the work with ORE, and I hope many more scholars and thinkers will help to expand and develop ORE.

What will this impact?

Through this book, I have explored what defines ORT. And from ORT, I have worked to define ORE by finding two theological legs: that we are called to be in, but not of the world, and that God calls us to be co-creators of creation.

That leads us to three practical outputs: We must have an active, co-creating community, utilize relational leadership, and always work with and toward radical inclusiveness.

This raises the last question of this book: Why at all is this needed? What will this actually impact?

Most Churches and denominations today find it more and more difficult to fill the pews. But it does not seem that people turn their back on religion or Christianity specifically.

In Denmark, the number of members of the Lutheran State Church has been consistently dropping. In 1986, 88.4% of Danes were members. In 2022, that had dropped to 73.2% and is still dropping. The dropout rate is so high that the state Church does not aim to gain more members but to lose fewer and celebrate when the drop is lower than last year. That is the mark of a bad crisis!

We do not have just as precise numbers for the free and evangelical Churches in Denmark, but much suggests the same trend is happening here. Fewer and fewer come to join Church communities, and more and more leave the communities. But why is that?

A study by the Barna Group sought to find reasons why the Millennial generation is leaving or unattracted to Church communities. This study resulted in a paper called *Making Space for Millenials - A Blueprint for Your Culture, Ministry, Leadership and Facilities.*[1] In this paper, they investigate, through both quantitative methods and with focus groups from different types of Churches in the United States, why the Millennial generation is giving up Churches.

The study by Barna Group concludes that there are five main characteristics of what millennials seek in Churches. These five are as follows:

Cultural discernment – engaging with the wider culture as a faith community to assess and respond biblically to its effects on human flourishing

Life-shaping relationships – consistent, long-term friendships with at least one older Christian adult who invests time and resources into their lives

A firsthand experience of Jesus – the confidence through seasons of doubt and pain that comes from having personally experienced God's revelation in Christ

Reverse mentoring – being valued for the knowledge, skills, and energy they can offer to older members of the community of faith

---

1. Barna Group, 'Making Space for Millenial - A Blueprint for Your Culture, Ministry, Leadership and Facilities', 2014.

Vocational discipleship – whole-life spiritual formation that includes understanding their work as a God-given calling[2]

These five main characteristics showed a clear mismatch between the leading idea in EPC Churches that we need to make the Church more appealing through better music, better lighting rigs, and fancy coffee machines. No, what millennials really need from their Church is true and authentic relationships within a community that actively seeks to change the world. According to this study, millennials seek communities of faith, where they can evolve and flourish in their calling and help others do so as well.

Following the publication of this research, the Christian blogger and public theologian Rachel Held Evans wrote a column for The Washington Post titled "Want millennials back in the pews? Stop trying to make Church 'cool.'"[3] The column was based on her escape from a "cool" Church and her way back to a more traditional Church. She brilliantly sums up why she returned to a more traditional and authentic Church:

> You can get a cup of coffee with your friends anywhere, but Church is the only place you can get ashes smudged on your forehead as a reminder of your mortality. You can be dazzled by a light show at a concert on any given weekend, but Church is the only place that fills a sanctuary with candlelight and hymns on Christmas Eve. You can snag all sorts of free swag for brand loyalty online, but Church is the only place where you are named a beloved

---

2. Barna Group, 6.

3. Rachel Held Evans, 'Want Millenials Back in the Pews? Stop Trying to Make Church "Cool"', 30 April 2015, https://www.washingtonpost.com/opinions/jesus-doesnt-tweet/ 2015/04/30/fb07ef1a-ed01-11e4-8666-a1d756d0218e_story.html.

child of God with a cold plunge into the water. You can share food with the hungry at any homeless shelter, but only the Church teaches that a shared meal brings us into the very presence of God.[4]

In truth, I believe Evans is speaking for an entire generation here. An entire generation is fed up with trendy Churches that try to use modern business tools and metaphors to create a service with the lowest possible doorstep, a service that is so bland that it makes the message easy and accessible to all but brings as little nutrients as a big-mac. I like to use the metaphor "7/11 Churches" for these trendy Churches because they try to be on every street corner; they all look the same, and there is no real food, only junk. The Barna study shows us that millennials want something different than just that.

The image is quite clear: To the millennial generation, the most important values for Church communities are **Community** (78%) over Privacy (22%), **Sanctuary** (77%) over Auditorium (23%), **Classic** (67%) over Trendy (33%), and **Quiet** (65%)) over Loud (35%).[5]

Perhaps apart from valuing community, millennials tend to choose everything that trendy EPC Churches are trying to move away from! Many EPC Churches seek to be trendy Churches in auditoriums with big light shows, smoke machines, and projectors. And they want to use big bands and create a concert atmosphere. But the majority of millennials, who are in focus here, just want a quiet, classic, and beautiful room with the opportunity for thought and reflection, but of course, still based on a loving,

---

4. Evans.

5. Barna Group, 'Designing Worship Spaces with Millennials in Mind', 5 November 2014, https://www.barna.com/research/designing-worship-spaces-with-millennials-in-mind/#.VS0dfxPF-4O.

supportive community. It is a very interesting perspective and hauntingly lines up with Evans' own experience.

Okay, so why this bit of background information?

ORE can be part of the solution here. Just start by looking at the five main characteristics of what millennials seek from their Churches, as quoted earlier, and the outline I have given on ORE.

Millennials seek cultural discernment, meaning that the Church should engage with the wider culture and respond biblically to its effects on human flourishing. ORE states that we are co-creators of creation and, thereby, the wider culture. ORE states that we should be part of building a culture based on the biblical view of God's essence as being love.

Millennials seek life-shaping relationships, meaning consistent, long-term friendships with someone who wants to invest time and resources into their lives. ORE states that all leadership, both in structured organizations and personal connections, must be based on relational leadership, which takes seriously the task of building up each other.

Millennials seek a firsthand experience of Jesus and a personal relationship with God. This fully aligns with ORT, which is the structure behind ORE. Therefore, the spiritual life of communities embracing ORE should always seek to mediate this personal, firsthand experience of God.

Millennials seek reverse mentoring, meaning that they should be valued for the knowledge, skills, and energy they can and want to offer older members of the community. Both in the aspects of relational leadership and radical inclusiveness, ORE should value all members and let them bring their charisms, experience, and energy to the table, both for building the community and for helping the older generation to develop.

Lastly, millennials seek vocational discipleship, meaning that there should be a whole-life spiritual formation, including understanding their work as a God-given calling. The focus of ORE on being co-creators helps to build vocational discipleship. Furthermore, the aspect of radical inclusiveness means that all are valued and can participate in being a disciple.

In all, embracing ORE would be exactly what the majority of millennials seek to find in a Church. I see that ORE is the best way to progress the Church and move it toward the 22nd century.

PART FOUR

Finishing Remarks

Forging the path ahead

This is not the end.

Well, it is the end of this book. That much is true.

But truly, this is not the end! This is just the beginning.

This is the beginning of what I see as THE most important conversations we must have these years.

This is the beginning of the conversation about how to make the Church relevant toward the 22nd century.

When I look at the church landscape today, most churches are afraid of progressing. Why? Why do we believe that theology and ecclesiology were better way back when? Why don't we engage in the society around us and keep up the process of evolving ever-better theology?

If we truly believe that God works through us Christians to create a better world, it is nonsense to believe the world was better yesterday than tomorrow.

God is in the process of building the Basileia right now.

Do we want to join in?

Do we want to explore the work together with God?

Do we have the courage and will to engage in the work of God?

We can actually progress our theology while holding onto fundamental beliefs. Progressivism and fundamentalism go hand in hand. We progress our thinking and understanding while holding on to fundamental beliefs.

Okay, I know the word fundamentalism scared some of you, especially the American readers. Let me just dwell on that word for a minute.

I usually call myself a progressive fundamentalist. I hold on to fundamental beliefs about God, as we can read in the stories of the Bible, and I hold on to the teachings of Christ. I hold on to the belief that God is love and the teachings of Christ that tell us to love our neighbor as much as we love God and ourselves.

Modern fundamentalism has a weird view of what the fundamentals are. They often infuse guns and xenophobia into their fundamental beliefs. They must read another Bible than I do.

Jesus calls us to love those estranged from society, to be xenophilic. And I have definitely never read of Jesus taking up arms.

What does Jesus say after one of the disciples draws a sword under his arrest in Gethsemane? Oh yes, that's right: "Put your sword back in its place, for all who draw the sword will die by the sword."[1]

Fundamentalism is not guns and xenophobia. It is love, charity, peace, and healing.

We need progressive fundamentalists.

And I truly believe that ORT is a good starting point.

I believe we, as Christians, must engage in the conversation of how we can progress into the 22nd century while holding onto the fundamentals. And I do not know of any better theological framework for that task than what we find in ORT.

I believe ORT can be the beginning of an ongoing conversation that will help Church leaders move the Church toward the 22nd century and keep up the good work of making the Church relevant anew.

Embracing ORE will help us to renew and reinvigorate Church communities, to again be an active force for good in the world, and to work in cooperation with the Divine.

Embracing ORE will truly help us to build the Basileia today.

---

1. Matt. 26:52

Bibliography

Barna Group. 'Designing Worship Spaces with Millennials in Mind', 5 November 2014. https://www.barna.com/research/designing-worship-spaces-with-millennials-in-mind/#.VS0dfxPF-4O.

———. 'Making Space for Millenial - A Blueprint for Your Culture, Ministry, Leadership and Facilities', 2014.

Barth, Karl. *Church Dogmatics, Volume IV, The Doctrine of Reconciliation*. Edinburgh: T & T Clark, 1956.

———. *The Doctrine of Creation. p. 3: Vol. 3. The Doctrine of Creation*. Vol. 3. London: Clark, 2004.

Benah, Sheila, and Yang Li. 'Examining the Relationship between Lean Supplier Relationship Management (LSRM) and Firm Performance: A Study on Manufacturing Companies in Ghana'. *Open Journal of Business and Management* 08, no. 06 (2020): 2423–50. https://doi.org/10.4236/ojbm.2020.86150.

Berg, C. *Oldgræsk-dansk Ordbog*. 3. udgave. Kbh.: Gyldendal, 2003.

Bible Hub. 'Strong's Greek: 932. Βασιλεία (Basileia)—Kingdom, Sovereignty, Royal Power', 2022. https://biblehub.com/greek/932.htm.

Boyd, Gregory A. *God of the Possible: A Biblical Introduction to the Open View of God*. Grand Rapids, Mich: Baker Books, 2000.

Buber, Martin. *I and Thou*. 46. print., 1. Touchstone ed. A Touchstone Book. New York: Simon & Schuster, 1996.

Caputo, John D. *The Folly of God: A Theology of the Unconditional*. Salem, Oregon: Polebridge Press, 2016.

Caulkin, Simon. 'Britain's Best Factories'. *Management Today*, no. November (1990): 60–89.

Clayton, Philip, and Tripp Fuller. *Transforming Christian Theology: For Church and Society*. Minneapolis: Fortress Press, 2010.

Cushing, Richard Cardinal. *The Servant Church*. Boston: Daughters of St. Paul, 1966.

Danmarks Statistik. 'NYT: Laveste antal udmeldinger af folkekirken i 15 år', 2022. https://www.dst.dk/da/Statistik/nyheder-analyser-publ/nyt/NytHtml?cid=38368.

Dulles, Avery. *Models of the Church*. Expanded ed. New York, NY: Image Books, 2002.

Evans, Rachel Held. 'Want Millennials Back in the Pews? Stop Trying to Make Church "Cool"', 30 April 2015. https://www.washingtonpost.com/opinions/jesus-doesnt-tweet/2015/04/30/fb07ef1a-ed01-11e4-8666-a1d756d0218e_story.html.

Gordon, Gabriel. *God Speaks: A Participatory Theology of Biblical Inspiration*, 2021.

Govier, Trudy. *Dilemmas of Trust*. Montreal ; Ithaca: McGill-Queen's University Press, 1998.

Hallbäck, Geert, and Hans Jørgen Lundager Jensen. *Gads bibel leksikon*. 2. udgave [1-Bindsudgave]. Kbh.: Gad, 2011.

Hearn, Roland, Sheri D. Kling, and Thomas Jay Oord, eds. *Open and Relational Leadership - Leading with Love*. USA: SacraSage, 2020.

Holtzen, William Curtis. *The God Who Trusts: A Relational Theology of Divine Faith, Hope, and Love*. Westmont: InterVarsity Press, 2019.

Kärkkäinen, Veli-Matti. *Introduction to Ecclesiology: Ecumenical, Historical & Global Perspectives*. Downers Grove, Ill: InterVarsity Press, 2002.

Karris, Mark Gregory. *Divine Echoes: Reconciling Prayer with the Uncontrolling Love of God*, 2018.

Keller, Catherine. *On the Mystery: Discerning Divinity in Process*. Minneapolis, MN: Fortress Press, 2008.

Komives, Susan R. *Exploring Leadership: For College Students Who Want to Make a Difference*. Third edition. San Francisco: Jossey-Bass, 2013.

Lewis, C. S. *Mere Christianity*. Überarbeitete und erweiterte Auflage, mit Neuer Einleitung der drei Bücher 'Broadcast Talks', 'Christian Behaviour' und 'Beyond Personality'. C. S. Lewis Signature Classics Edition. London: HarperCollins, 2016.

Loomer, Bernard. 'Two Conceptions of Power'. *Process Studies* 6, no. 1 (1976): 5–32.

Lubac, Henri de. *Catholicism: Christ and the Common Destiny of Man.* San Francisco: Ignatius Press, 1988.

Mayer, John. *Love Is a Verb.* Born and Raised. Columbia Records, 2012.

McGrath, Alister E., ed. *The Blackwell Encyclopedia of Modern Christian Thought.* Reprinted. Oxford: Blackwell, 2000.

Mesle, C. Robert. *Process Theology: A Basic Introduction.* St. Louis, Mo: Chalice Press, 1993.

———. *Process-Relational Philosophy: An Introduction to Alfred North Whitehead.* West Conshohocken, Pa: Templeton Foundation Press, 2008.

Moltmann, Jürgen. 'God's Kenosis in the Creation and Consummation of the World'. In *The Work of Love: Creation as Kenosis,* edited by John Polkinghorne. Eerdmans, 2001.

———. *The Church in the Power of the Spirit: A Contribution to Messianic Ecclesiology.* 1st Fortress Press ed. Minneapolis: Fortress Press, 1993.

———. *The Spirit of Life: A Universal Affirmation.* Minneapolis: Fortress Press, 2001.

Mortensen, Jonas. *Det fælles bedste: introduktion til personalismen.* Edited by Steffen Boeskov and Leif E. Kristensen. 1. udgave, 1. oplag. Frederiksværk: Boedal, 2012.

Müller, Mogens. *Kommentar til Matthæusevangeliet.* Dansk kommentar til Det nye Testamente 3. Århus: Aarhus Universitetsforl, 2000.

Oord, Thomas Jay. *Open and Relational Theology: An Introduction to Life-Changing Ideas.* Grasmere, Idaho: SacraSage Press, 2021.

———. *Pluriform Love: An Open and Relational Theology of Well-Being.* Sacra Sage Press, 2022.

———. *The Death of Omnipotence and Birth of Amipotence.* U.S.A.: Sacrasage Press, 2023.

———. *The Nature of Love: A Theology.* St. Louis: Chalice Press, 2010.

———. *The Uncontrolling Love of God: An Open and Relational Account of Providence.* Downers Grove, Illinois: InterVarsity Press, 2015.

Pinnock, Clark H. *Flame of Love: A Theology of the Holy Spirit.* Downers Grove, Ill: InterVarsity Press, 1996.

─────. *Most Moved Mover: A Theology of God's Openness.* Place of publication not identified: WIPF & STOCK Publishers, 2019.

─────, ed. *The Openness of God: A Biblical Challenge to the Traditional Understanding of God.* Downers Grove, Ill: InterVarsity Press, 1994.

Rice, Richard. *The Openness of God: The Relationship of Divine Foreknowledge and Human Free Will.* Horizon. Nashville, TN: Review and Herald Pub. Association, 1980.

Rivington, F. *The British Critic and Quarterly Theological Review*, 1837.

Sanders, John. *Embracing Prodigals: Overcoming Authoritative Religion by Embodying Jesus' Nurturing Grace.* Eugene, OR: Cascade Books, 2020.

─────. *The God Who Risks: A Theology of Divine Providence.* 2nd ed., Rev. ed. Downers Grove, Ill: IVP Academic, 2007.

Swinton, John, and Harriet Mowatt. *Practical Theology and Qualitative Research.* 2., rev. Ed. London: SCM, 2016.

Volf, Miroslav. 'A Protestant Response to "We Are the Church: New Congregationalism"'. *Concilium*, no. 3 (1996).

Whitehead, Alfred North. *Process and Reality: An Essay in Cosmology Gifford Lectures Delivered in the University of Edinburgh during the Session 1927-28.* Corr. ed. New York London: the Free press, 1978.

Youtz, Herbet A. 'Three Conceptions of God'. *American Journal of Theology* II (1907): 428–53.

About the Author

U lrick Dam is a Danish theologian, accomplished author, speaker, and an acclaimed leadership advisor. Ulrick specializes in assisting both churches and corporations in cultivating vibrant cultures where the pillars of relationships and empathy stand tall. When he steps away from his professional pursuits, Ulrick retreats to the Danish countryside, where he shares his life with his wife and son. If you ever want to get him a gift, you'll never go wrong with a great book or some delicious coffee beans.